SCOTT FORESMAN · ADDISON WESLEY

Volume 2A Topics 9–12

Authors

Randall I. Charles
Professor Emeritus
Department of Mathematics
San Jose State University
San Jose, California

Jennifer Bay-Williams
Professor of Mathematics Education
College of Education and Human
Development
University of Louisville
Louisville, Kentucky

Robert Q. Berry, III
Associate Professor of
Mathematics Education
Department of Curriculum,
Instruction and Special Education
University of Virginia
Charlottesville, Virginia

Janet H. Caldwell
Professor of Mathematics
Rowan University
Glassboro, New Jersey

Zachary Champagne
Assistant in Research
Florida Center for Research in Science,
Technology, Engineering, and
Mathematics (FCR-STEM)
Jacksonville, Florida

Juanita Copley
Professor Emerita, College of Education
University of Houston
Houston, Texas

Warren Crown
Professor Emeritus of Mathematics
Education
Graduate School of Education
Rutgers University
New Brunswick, New Jersey

Francis (Skip) Fennell
L. Stanley Bowlsbey Professor
of Education and Graduate and
Professional Studies
McDaniel College
Westminster, Maryland

Karen Karp
Professor of Mathematics Education
Department of Early Childhood and
Elementary Education
University of Louisville
Louisville, Kentucky

Stuart J. Murphy
Visual Learning Specialist
Boston, Massachusetts

Jane F. Schielack
Professor of Mathematics
Associate Dean for Assessment and
Pre K–12 Education, College of Science
Texas A&M University
College Station, Texas

Jennifer M. Suh
Associate Professor for
Mathematics Education
George Mason University
Fairfax, Virginia

Jonathan A. Wray
Mathematics Instructional Facilitator
Howard County Public Schools
Ellicott City, Maryland

PEARSON

Glenview, Illinois   Boston, Massachusetts   Chandler, Arizona   New York, New York

MW00806794

Mathematicians

Roger Howe
Professor of Mathematics
Yale University
New Haven, Connecticut

Gary Lippman
Professor of Mathematics and
Computer Science
California State University, East Bay
Hayward, California

ELL Consultants

Janice R. Corona
Independent Education Consultant
Dallas, Texas

Jim Cummins
Professor
The University of Toronto
Toronto, Canada

Debbie Crisco
Math Coach
Beebe Public Schools
Beebe, Arkansas

Kathleen A. Cuff
Teacher
Kings Park Central School District
Kings Park, New York

Erika Doyle
Math and Science Coordinator
Richland School District
Richland, Washington

Reviewers

Susan Jarvis
Math and Science Curriculum Coordinator
Ocean Springs Schools
Ocean Springs, Mississippi

ISBN-13: 978-0-328-93060-9
ISBN-10:   0-328-93060-1

3 18

> You'll be using these digital resources throughout the year!

Digital Resources

Go to PearsonRealize.com

MP

Math Practices Animations to play anytime

Solve

Solve & Share problems plus math tools

Learn

Visual Learning Animation Plus with animation, interaction, and math tools

Glossary

Animated Glossary in English and Spanish

Tools

Math Tools to help you understand

Assessment

Quick Check for each lesson

Help

Another Look Homework Video for extra help

Games

Math Games to help you learn

eText

Student Edition online

ACTIVe-book

Student Edition online for showing your work

PEARSON realize. Everything you need for math anytime, anywhere

Contents

KEY

- Numbers: Concepts and Counting
- Operations and Algebra
- Numbers and Computation
- Measurement and Data
- Geometry

Digital Resources at PearsonRealize.com

And remember your eText is available at PearsonRealize.com!

TOPICS

PearsonRealize.com

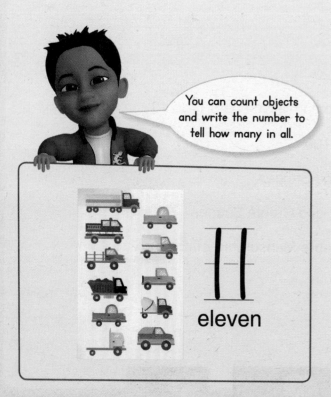

You can count objects and write the number to tell how many in all.

eleven

TOPIC 9
Count Numbers to 20

The equation tells how many cubes in all.

$$10 + 2 = 12$$

TOPIC 10
Compose and Decompose Numbers 11 to 19

PearsonRealize.com

TOPIC 11
Count Numbers to 100

You can use part of a hundred chart to count and find patterns.

1	2	3	4	5	6	7	8	9	10
11	12	13	14	15	16	17	18	19	20
21	22	23	24	25	26	27	28	29	30

TOPIC 12
Identify and Describe Shapes

There are flat and solid objects in our environment. The notebook paper and envelope are flat. The cup and tissue box are solid.

TOPIC 13
Analyze, Compare, and Create Shapes

The side of this cube is a square.

Contents

TOPIC 14
Describe and Compare Measurable Attributes

You can compare the sizes of different objects.

Shorter

STEP UP to Grade 1

These lessons help prepare you for Grade 1.

Problem Solving Handbook

Math Practices

1. Make sense of problems and persevere in solving them.

2. Reason abstractly and quantitatively.

3. Construct viable arguments and critique the reasoning of others.

4. Model with mathematics.

5. Use appropriate tools strategically.

6. Attend to precision.

7. Look for and make use of structure.

8. Look for and express regularity in repeated reasoning.

There are good Thinking Habits for each of these math practices.

1 # Make sense of problems and persevere in solving them.

My plan was to count the bees. The last number I counted was the total number of bees.

Good math thinkers know what the problem is about. They have a plan to solve it. They keep trying if they get stuck.

How many bees are there in all? How do you know?

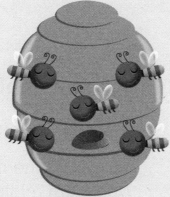

Thinking Habits

What do I need to find?

What do I know?

What's my plan for solving the problem?

What else can I try if I get stuck?

How can I check that my solution make sense?

2 Reason abstractly and quantitatively.

This problem is about the number 4. I can show 4 in a different way to solve the problem.

Good math thinkers know how to think about words and numbers to solve problems.

Daniel sees 4 frogs. He wants to draw 4 dragonflies in a different arrangement. What other way can he show the number 4?

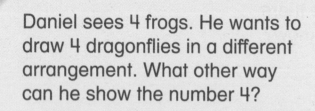

4
4

Thinking Habits

What do the numbers stand for?

How are the numbers in the problem related?

How can I show a word problem using pictures or numbers?

How can I use a word problem to show what an equation means?

MP

3 Construct viable arguments and critique the reasoning of others.

Good math thinkers use math to explain why they are right. They talk about math that others do, too.

I used a picture and words to explain my thinking.

How is the second box like the first box?
Explain your answer.

I counted the stars. I counted the counters. Both boxes have 3 things.

Thinking Habits

How can I use math to explain my work?

Am I using numbers and symbols correctly?

Is my explanation clear?

What questions can I ask to understand other people's thinking?

Are there mistakes in other people's thinking?

Can I improve other people's thinking?

4 Model with mathematics.

MP

I used the colored boxes to show the correct answer.

Good math thinkers use math they know to show and solve problems.

Place 2 counters in the nest. Peeps found these worms for her babies. How can you use the model below the nest to show how many worms Peeps found?

Thinking Habits

How can I use the math I know to help solve this problem?

Can I use a drawing, diagram, table, or objects to show the problem?

Can I write an equation to show the problem?

5 Use appropriate tools strategically.

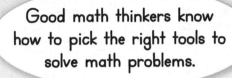

Good math thinkers know how to pick the right tools to solve math problems.

I chose counters to solve the problem.

How many leaves are there in all? Use counters, connecting cubes, or other objects to show how many, and then write the number to tell how many.

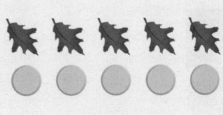

5

Thinking Habits

Which tools can I use?

Is there a different tool I could use?

Am I using the tool correctly?

6 Attend to precision.

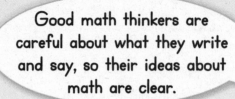

Good math thinkers are careful about what they write and say, so their ideas about math are clear.

I was careful when I counted and colored.

Each bird found some worms for her babies. Did they find the same number or different numbers of worms? Color the boxes to show how you know.

Thinking Habits

Am I using numbers, units, and symbols correctly?

Am I using the correct definitions?

Is my answer clear?

7 Look for and make use of structure.

Good math thinkers look for patterns in math to help solve problems.

I found a pattern.

How can you tell how many objects you see without counting first?
Explain how you know you are right.

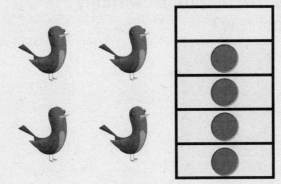

Thinking Habits

Is there a pattern?

How can I describe the pattern?

Can I break the problem into simpler parts?

MP 8 Look for and express regularity in repeated reasoning.

I know that the 1 more repeats. That helped me solve the problem.

Good math thinkers look for things that repeat in a problem. They use what they learn from one problem to help them solve other problems.

The first row has 1 counter colored. Each row has 1 more counter than the row before. How many counters will be in the last row?

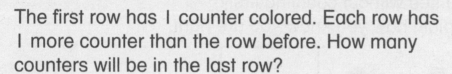

1

2

Thinking Habits

Does something repeat in the problem?

How can the solution help me solve another problem?

Problem Solving Handbook

Problem Solving Guide

These questions can help you solve problems.

Make Sense of the Problem

Reason
- What do I need to find?
- What given information can I use?
- How are the quantities related?

Think About Similar Problems
- Have I solved problems like this before?

Persevere in Solving the Problem

Model with Math
- How can I use the math I know?
- How can I show the problem?
- Is there a pattern I can use?

Use Appropriate Tools
- What math tools could I use?
- How can I use those tools?

Check the Answer

Make Sense of the Answer
- Is my answer reasonable?

Check for Precision
- Did I check my work?
- Is my answer clear?
- Is my explanation clear?

Some Ways to Show Problems
- Draw a Picture
- Write an Equation

Some Math Tools
- Objects
- Technology
- Paper and Pencil

Problem Solving Handbook

Problem Solving Recording Sheet

This sheet helps you organize your work.

Name **Gretchen**

Teaching Tool
1

Problem Solving Recording Sheet

Problem:
5 birds are on a fence.
2 birds fly away.
How many birds are left?

MAKE SENSE OF THE PROBLEM

Need to Find	**Given**
I need to find how many birds are left.	5 birds are on a fence. 2 birds fly away.

PERSEVERE IN SOLVING THE PROBLEM

Some Ways to Represent Problems
☑ Draw a Picture
☑ Write an Equation

Some Math Tools
☐ Objects
☐ Technology
☑ Paper and Pencil

Solution and Answer

3 birds
5 − 2 = 3

CHECK THE ANSWER

I listened to the problem again. I checked my picture and counted the birds that were left, 3 birds. My answer is correct.

 TT1

TOPIC 9 Count Numbers to 20

Essential Question: How can numbers to 20 be counted, read, written, and pictured to tell how many?

Digital Resources

Solve Learn Glossary

Tools Assessment Help Games

Math and Science Project: What Can We Get From Plants?

Directions Read the character speech bubbles to students. **Find Out!** Have students find out ways plants impact and change their environment. Say: *Talk to friends and relatives about what plants do for the environment. Ask them how humans and animals use things in the environment, such as plants, to meet their needs.* **Journal: Make a Poster** Have students make a poster. Ask them to draw some ways that plants can provide food and shelter for animals and humans. Finally, have students draw an orange tree with 15 oranges.

Topic 9

five hundred seven **507**

Name _____

★ 1

$$5 + 4 = 9$$

$$5 - 4 = 1$$

🍎 2

$$6 - 3 = 3$$

🔄 3

$$7 - 4 = 3$$

♥ 4

5   15   10

✋ 5

_____   _____   _____

- - - - - + - - - - - = - - - - -

_____   _____   _____

Directions Have students: ★ draw a circle around the equation that shows addition; 🍎 draw a circle around the minus sign; 🔄 draw a circle around the difference; ♥ draw a circle around the correct number of counters shown; ✋ count the red counters, count the yellow counters, and then write the equation to find the sum.

     Topic 9

My Word Cards

Directions Have students cut out the vocabulary cards. Read the front of the card, and then ask them to explain what the word or phrase means.

A-Z Glossary

eleven	twelve	thirteen
fourteen	fifteen	sixteen

My Word Cards

Directions Review the definitions and have students study the cards. Extend learning by having students draw pictures for each word on a separate piece of paper.

13

Point to the apples.
Say: *There are 13 apples.*

12

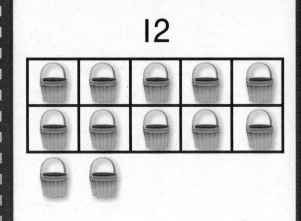

Point to the pails.
Say: *There are 12 pails.*

11

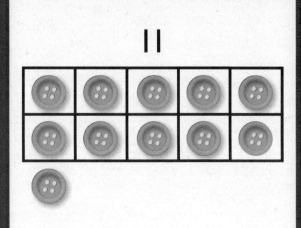

Point to the buttons.
Say: *There are 11 buttons.*

16

Point to the pigs.
Say: *There are 16 pigs.*

15

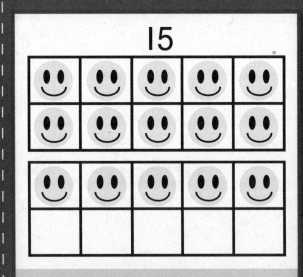

Point to the smiley faces.
Say: *There are 15 smiley faces.*

14

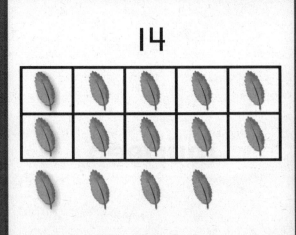

Point to the leaves.
Say: *There are 14 leaves.*

My Word Cards

Directions Have students cut out the vocabulary cards. Read the front of the card, and then ask them to explain what the word or phrase means.

seventeen	**eighteen**	**nineteen**
twenty	**row**	

My Word Cards

Directions Review the definitions and have students study the cards. Extend learning by having students draw pictures for each word on a separate piece of paper.

19

Point to the hats.
Say: *There are 19 hats.*

18

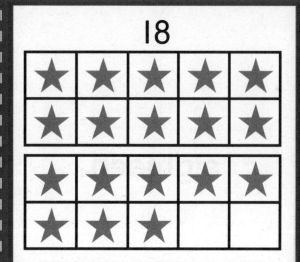

Point to the stars.
Say: *There are 18 stars.*

17

Point to the moons.
Say: *There are 17 moons.*

1	2	3	4	5
11	12	13	14	15
21	22	23	24	25
31	32	33	34	35

Point to the circled row.
Say: *This is a **row**. Rows go side to side.*

20

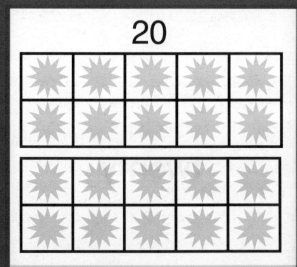

Point to the suns.
Say: *There are 20 suns.*

Name _____

I can ...
count and write the numbers
11 and 12.

I can also model
with math.

Directions Say: *Carlos has a collection of toy cars. How can Carlos show the number of cars he has? Use counters, and then draw them to show one way.*

Digital Resources at PearsonRealize.com

| |

eleven

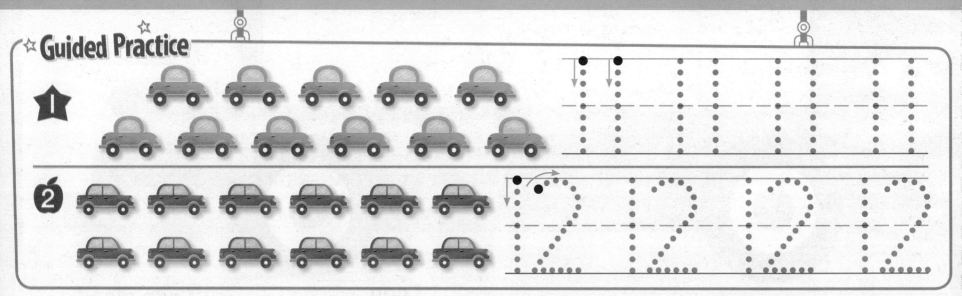

☆ **Guided Practice**

1

2

Directions ⭐ and ② Have students count the cars in each group, and then practice writing the number that tells how many.

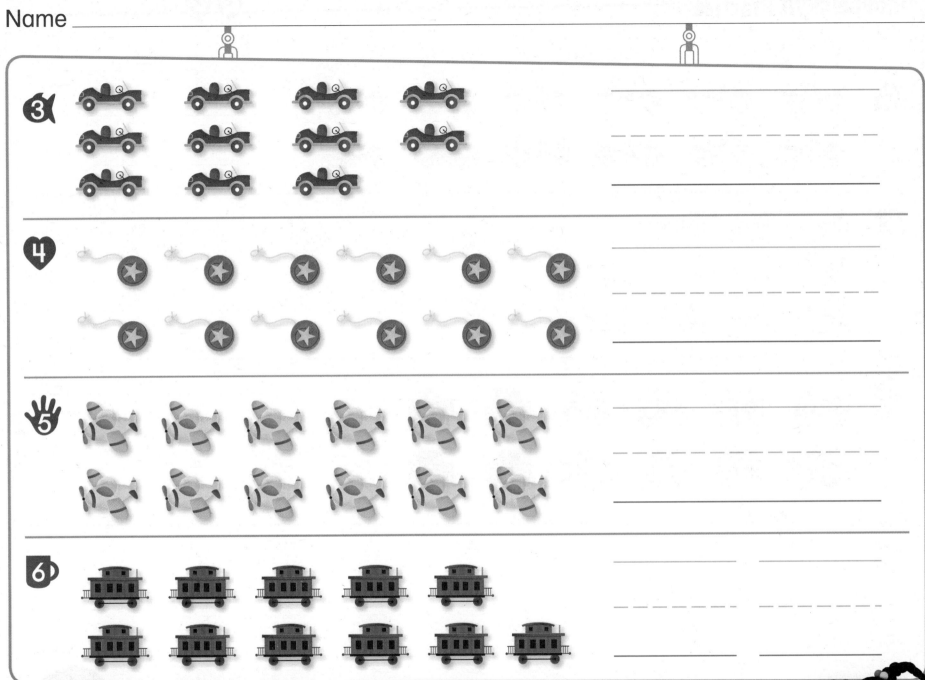

3

4

5

6

Directions 🛈–✋ Have students count the toys in each group, and then practice writing the number that tells how many. 🛈 **Number Sense** Have students count the train cars, write the number to tell how many, and then write the number that comes after it.

Independent Practice

7

_____

8

_____

9

_____

10

_____

Directions 7—9 Have students count the toys in each group, and then practice writing the number that tells how many. 10 **Higher Order Thinking** Have students draw 11 toys, and then practice writing the number that tells how many.

Name _____

Another Look!

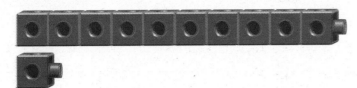

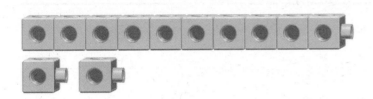

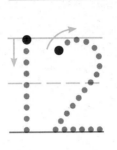

HOME ACTIVITY Draw groups of 11 and 12 circles, each on a separate index card. Have your child write the correct number on the back of each card. Then use the cards to practice counting and writing the numbers 11 and 12.

 1

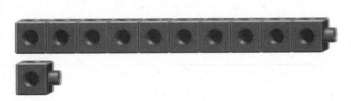

_____

- - - - - - - - -

_____

 2

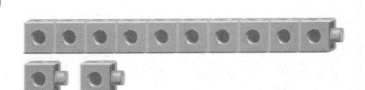

- - - - - - - - -

- - - - - - - - -

_____

Directions Say: *Count the connecting cubes, and then write the number to tell how many.* ★ and ② Have students count the connecting cubes, and then write the number to tell how many.

3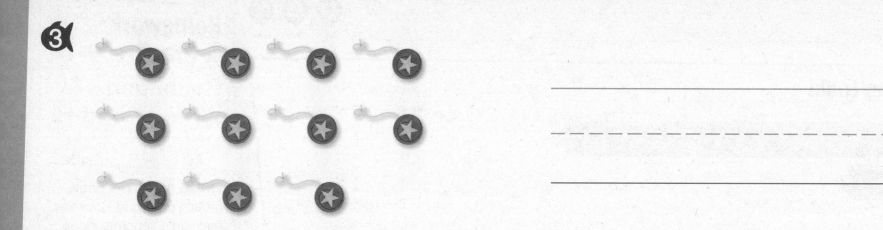

_____

- - - - - - - - - - - - -

_____

4

_____

- - - - - - - - - - - - -

_____

5

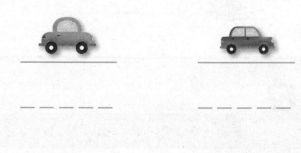

_____   _____

- - - - - - - - -   - - - - - - - - -

_____   _____

Directions ❸ Have students count the yo-yos, and then practice writing the number that tells how many. ❹ **Higher Order Thinking** Have students draw 12 toys, and then practice writing the number that tells how many. ❺ **Higher Order Thinking** Have students count each group of cars, and then write the numbers to tell how many.

© Pearson Education, Inc. K

Solve & Share

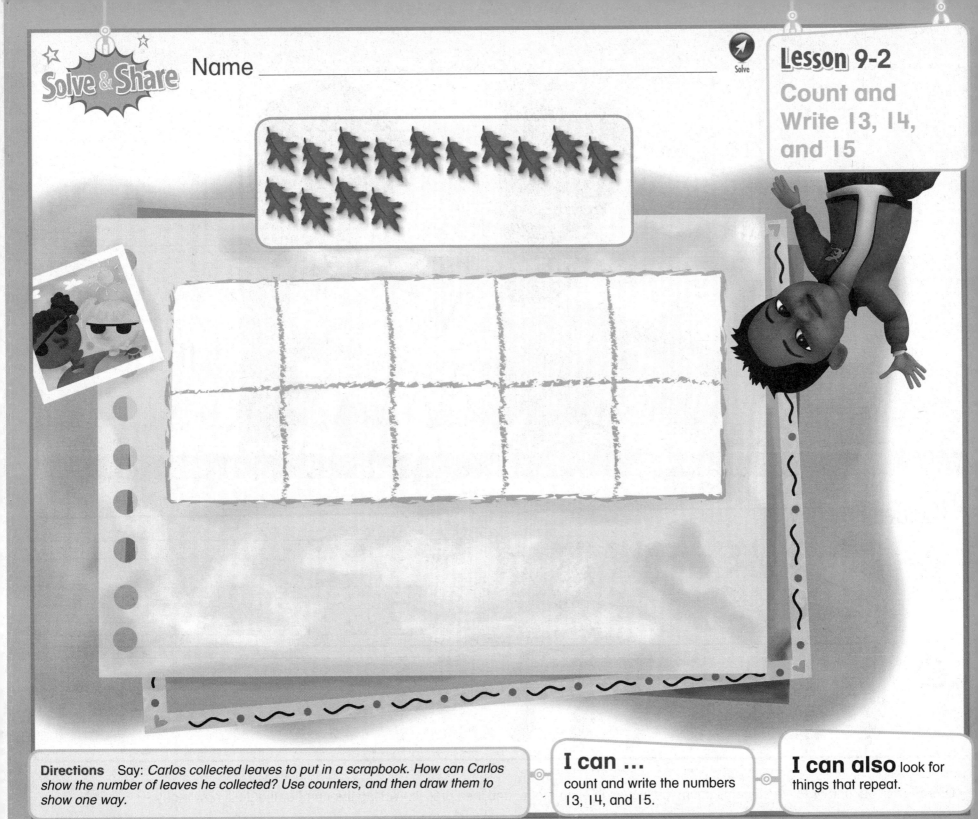

Directions Say: *Carlos collected leaves to put in a scrapbook. How can Carlos show the number of leaves he collected? Use counters, and then draw them to show one way.*

I can ...
count and write the numbers 13, 14, and 15.

I can also look for things that repeat.

Topic 9 | Lesson 2
Digital Resources at PearsonRealize.com
five hundred nineteen **519**

13

thirteen

☆ Guided Practice

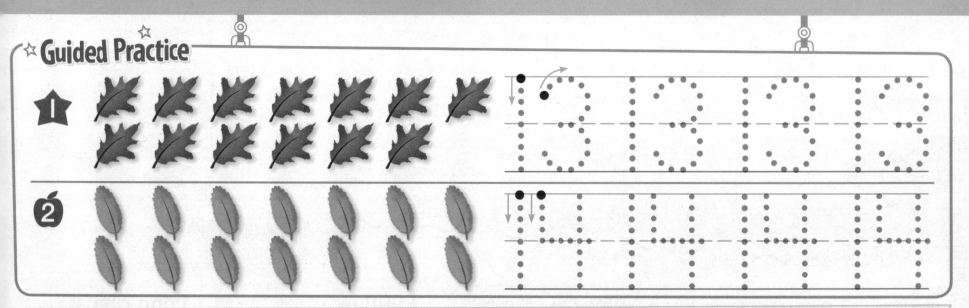

Directions ⭐ and 🍎 Have students count the leaves in each group, and then practice writing the number that tells how many.

Name _____

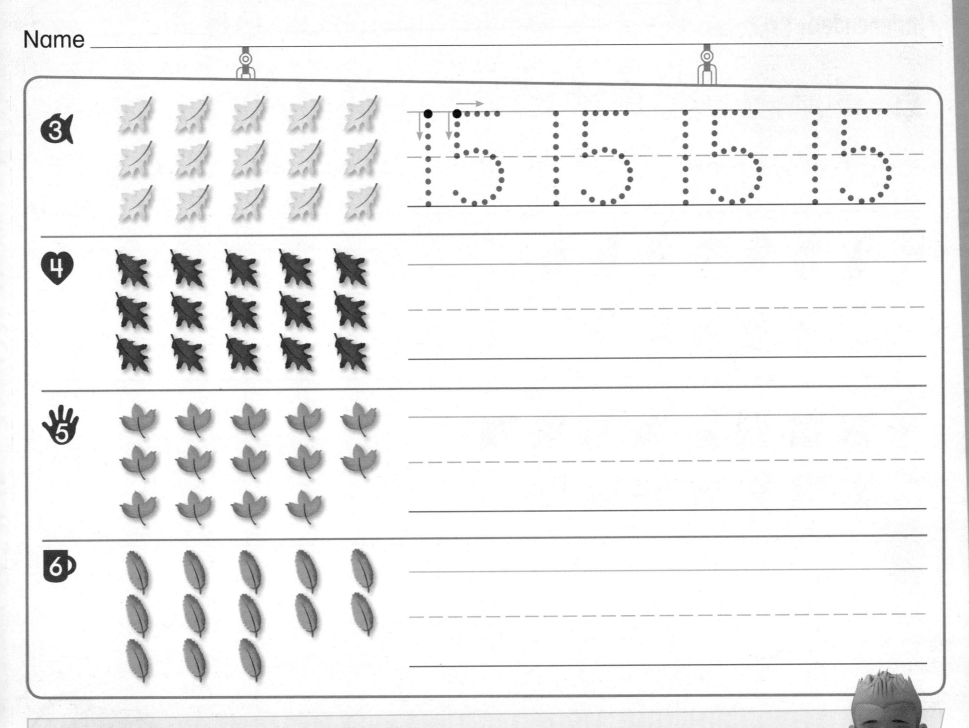

3 15 15 15 15 15

4

5

6

Directions **3**–**5** Have students count the leaves in each group, and then practice writing the number that tells how many.
6 **Math and Science** Say: *Trees use their leaves to turn sunlight into food.* Have students count the green leaves, and then practice writing the number that tells how many.

Topic 9 | Lesson 2

five hundred twenty-one **521**

Independent Practice

7

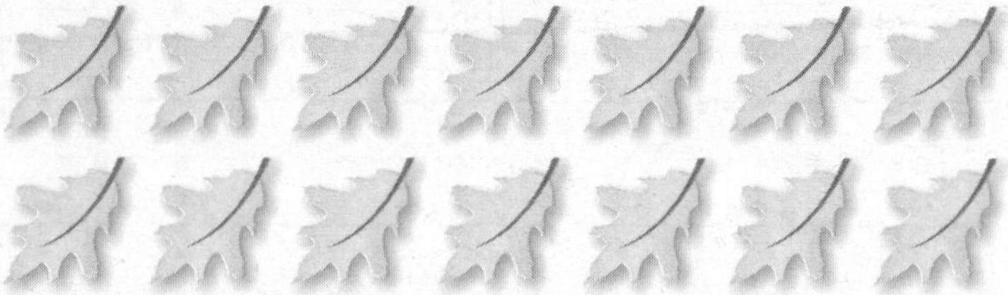

8

9

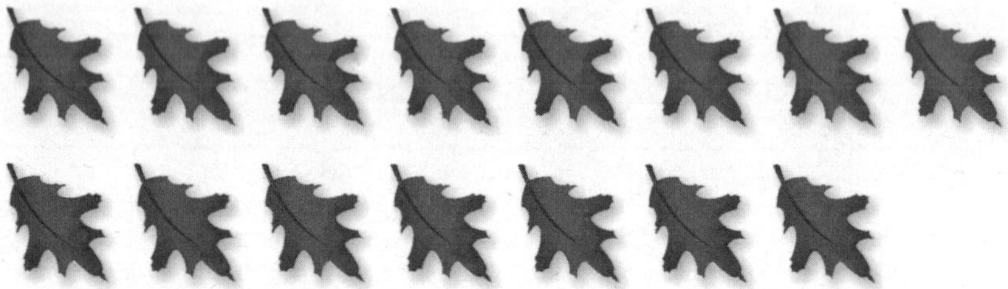

10

© Pearson Education, Inc. K

Directions 7–9 Have students count the leaves in each group, and then practice writing the number that tells how many. 10 **Higher Order Thinking** Have students draw 14 leaves, and then practice writing the number that tells how many.

522 five hundred twenty-two

Name _____

Another Look!

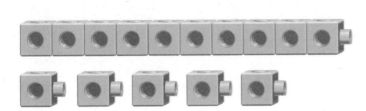

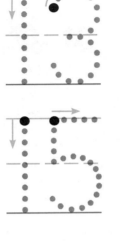

HOME ACTIVITY Have your child write the numbers 13, 14, and 15 on 3 index cards. Show your child groups of 13, 14, and 15 objects. Have her or him count the objects in each group, say the numbers, and match the number cards to the groups.

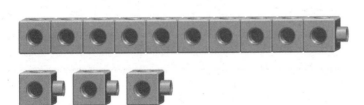

_ _ _ _ _ _

_____

_____

_ _ _ _ _ _

_____

Directions Say: *Count the connecting cubes, and then write the number to tell how many.* and Have students count the connecting cubes, and then write the number to tell how many.

3

_____

- - - - - - - - - - - - - - - - - - -

_____

4

_____

- - - - - - - - - - - - - - - - - - -

_____

5

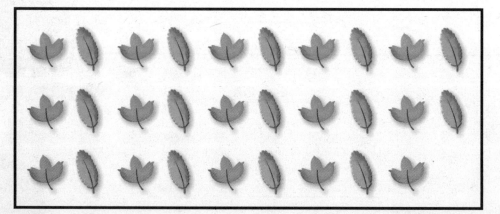

_____   _____

- - - - -   - - - - -

_____   _____

Directions ❸ Have students count the leaves, and then practice writing the number that tells how many.
❹ **Higher Order Thinking** Have students draw 13 leaves, and then practice writing the number that tells how many.
❺ **Higher Order Thinking** Have students count each group of leaves, and then write the numbers to tell how many.

© Pearson Education, Inc. K   **Topic 9** | Lesson 2

Name _____

Solve

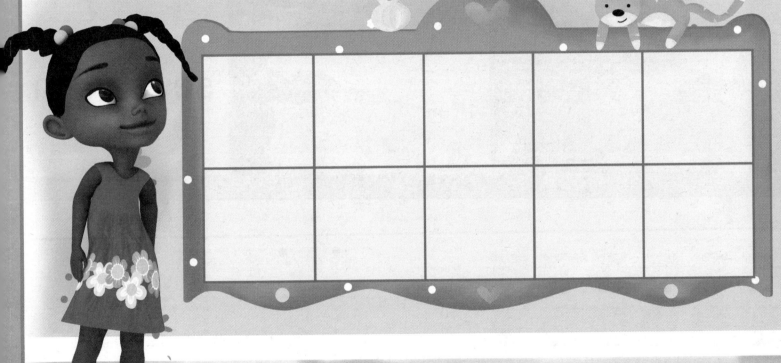

Directions Say: *Jada has a collection of piggy banks. How can Carlos show the number of piggy banks Jada has? Use counters, and then draw them to show one way.*

I can ...
count and write the numbers 16 and 17.

I can also model with math.

17

seventeen

☆ Guided Practice

1

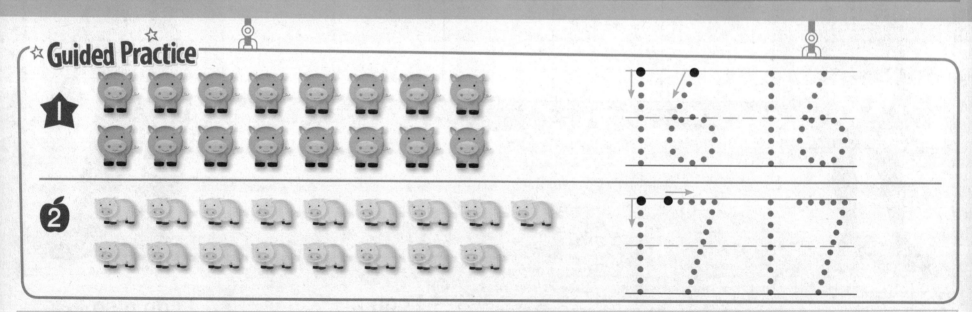

2

Directions 1 and 2 Have students count the piggy banks in each group, and then practice writing the number that tells how many.

© Pearson Education, Inc. K

Name _____

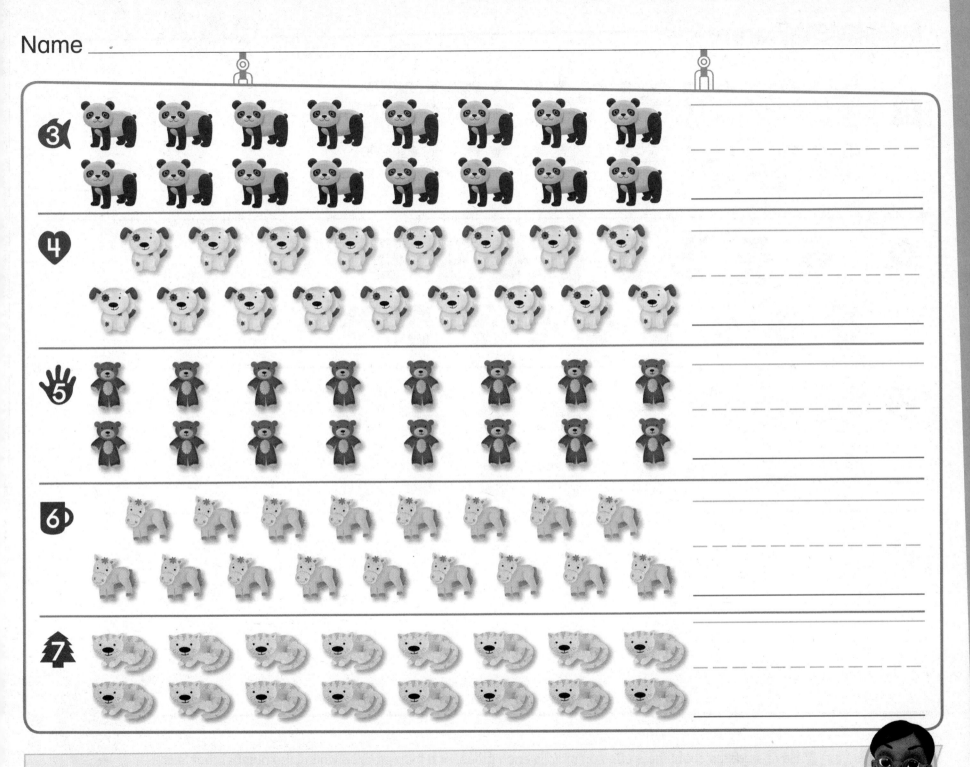

Directions 3–7 Have students count the stuffed animals in each group, and then practice writing the number that tells how many.

Topic 9 | Lesson 3

five hundred twenty-seven **527**

Independent Practice

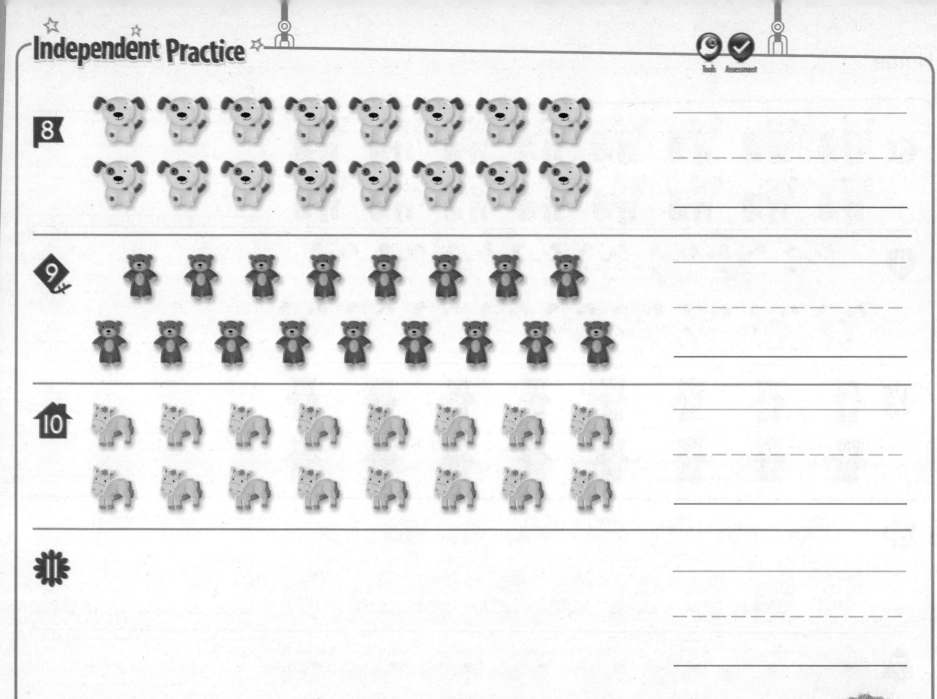

8 _____

_____

9 _____

_____

10 _____

_____

_____

_____

Directions 🟦–🟥 Have students count the stuffed animals in each group, and then practice writing the number that tells how many. ❋ **Higher Order Thinking** Have students draw 17 balls, and then practice writing the number that tells how many.

528 five hundred twenty-eight © Pearson Education, Inc. K **Topic 9** | Lesson 3

Name _____

Another Look!

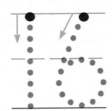

HOME ACTIVITY Have your child write the numbers 16 and 17 on 2 index cards. Show your child groups of 16 and 17 objects. Have him or her count the objects, say the numbers, and match the number cards to the groups.

 1

_ _ _ _ _ _ _ _

 2

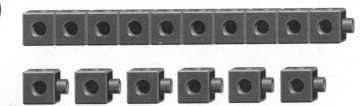

_ _ _ _ _ _ _ _

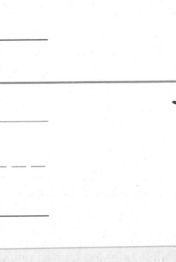

Directions Say: *Count the connecting cubes, and then write the number to tell how many.* **1** and **2** Have students count the connecting cubes, and then write the number to tell how many.

3

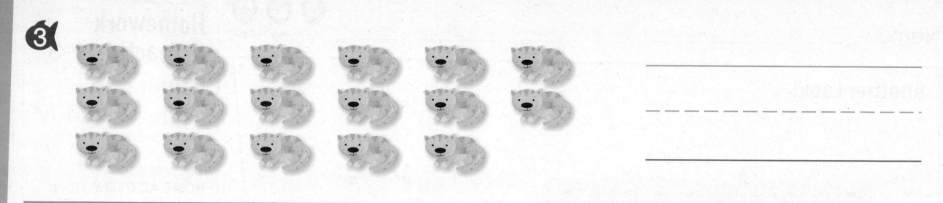

_____

- - - - - - - - - - -

_____

4

_____

- - - - - - - - - - -

_____

5 🖐

- - - - - - - - - - -   - - - - - - - - - -

_____

Directions ✦ Have students count the stuffed animals, and then practice writing the number that tells how many.
✦ **Higher Order Thinking** Have students draw 16 balls, and then practice writing the number that tells how many.
🖐 **Higher Order Thinking** Have students count each group of piggy banks, and then write the numbers to tell how many.

Solve & Share

Name _____

Directions Say: *Carlos has a collection of bird stickers in his sticker album. How can Carlos show the number of bird stickers he has? Use counters, and then draw them to show one way.*

I can ...
count and write the numbers 18, 19, and 20.

I can also use math tools correctly.

19

nineteen

Guided Practice

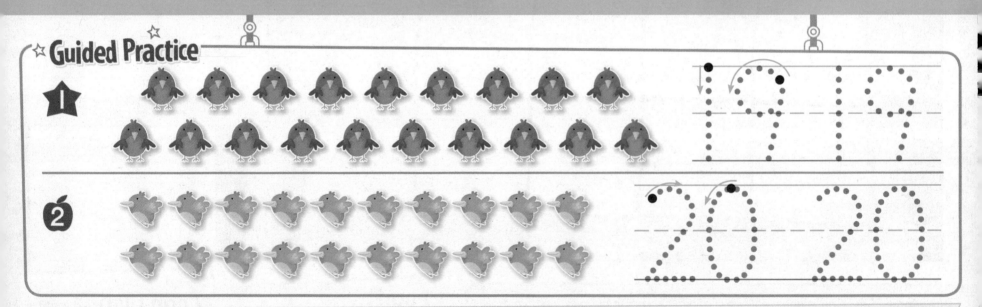

1

2

Directions ⭐ and ❷ Have students count the bird stickers in each group, and then practice writing the number that tells how many.

Name _____

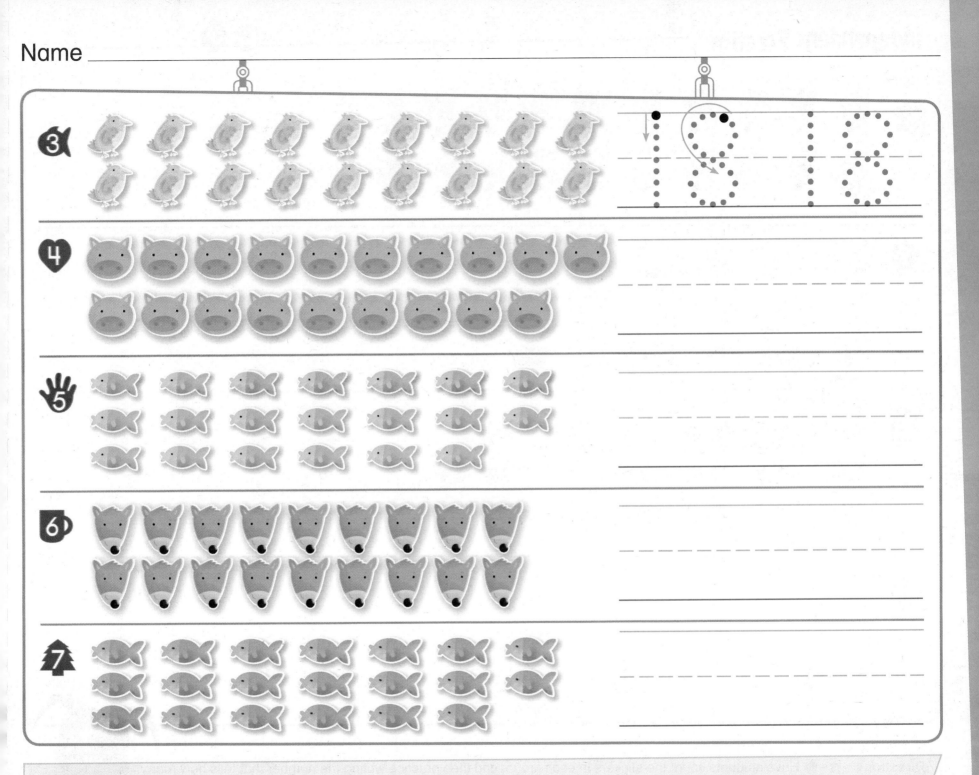

Directions ⬥–7 Have students count the stickers in each group, and then practice writing the number that tells how many.

Topic 9 | Lesson 4

five hundred thirty-three **533**

Independent Practice

Tools Assessment

8

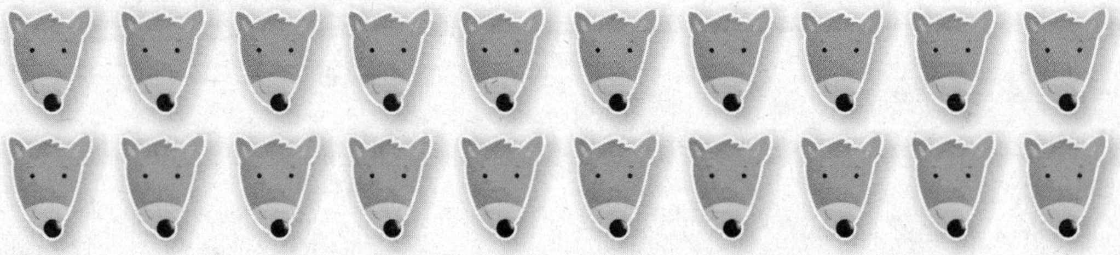

9

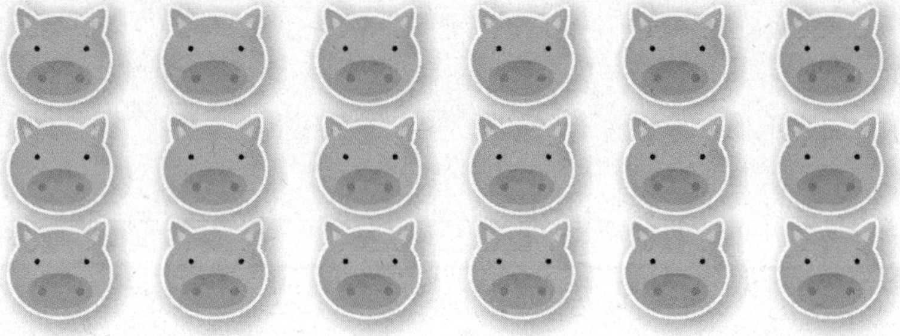

10

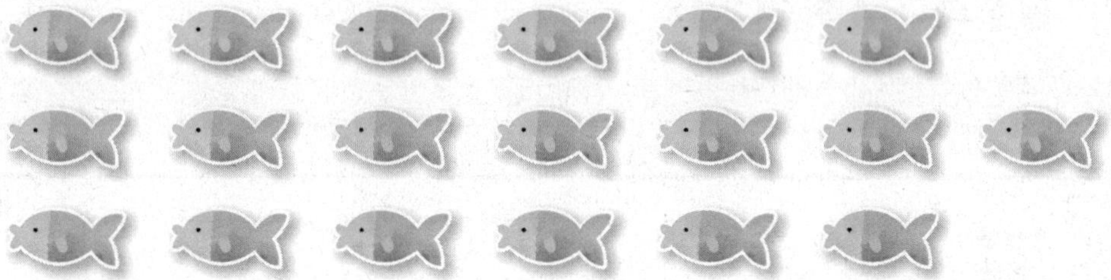

11

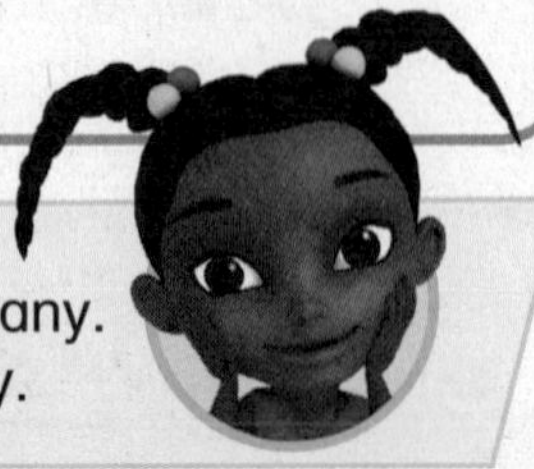

Directions 8–10 Have students count the stickers in each group, and then practice writing the number that tells how many. 11 **Higher Order Thinking** Have students draw 20 bug stickers, and then practice writing the number that tells how many.

Name _____

Another Look!

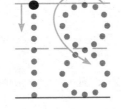

HOME ACTIVITY Have your child draw 18 objects, and then write the number 18 below the group of objects. Repeat for the numbers 19 and 20.

_____

- - - - - - - -

_____

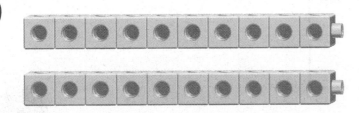

_____

- - - - - - - -

_____

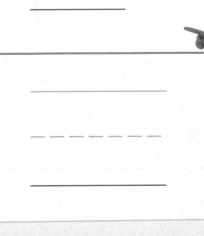

Directions Say: *Count the connecting cubes, and then write the number to tell how many.* ⭐ and ② Have students count the connecting cubes, and then write the number to tell how many.

3

_____

- - - - - - - - - - - - - -

_____

4

_____

- - - - - - - - - - - - - -

_____

5

_____

- - - - - - - - - - - - - -

_____

Directions **3** Have students count the stickers, and then practice writing the number that tells how many.
4 Vocabulary Have students draw **nineteen** worm stickers, and then practice writing the number that tells how many.
5 Higher Order Thinking Have students count each group of stickers, and then write the numbers to tell how many.

★ ☆ ★
Solve & Share

Solve

Start

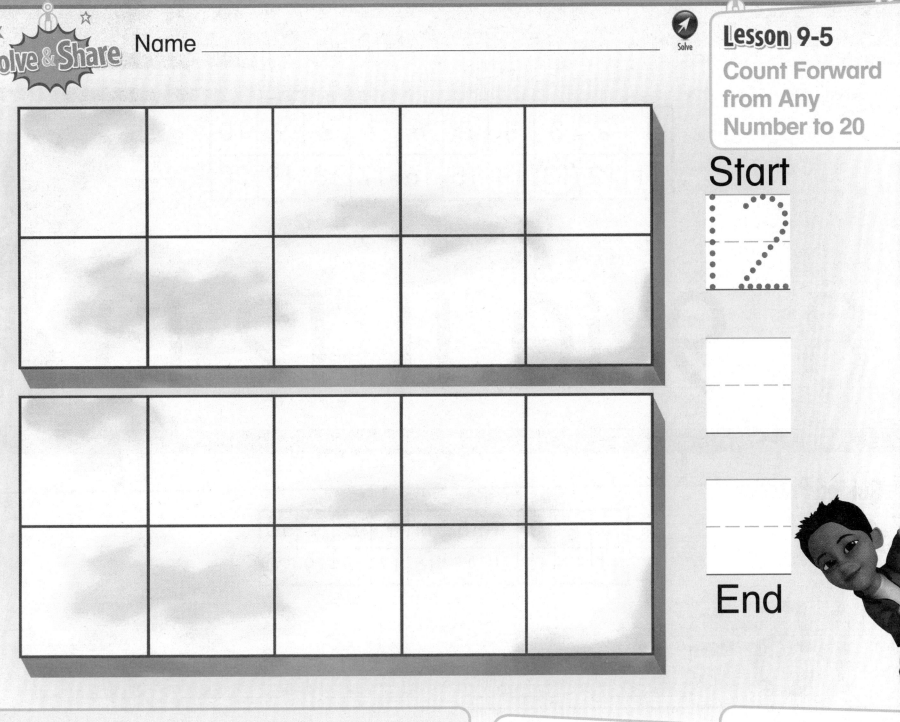

End

Directions Say: *Put 12 counters on the double ten-frame. Write the number to tell how many. Put 1 more counter on the double ten-frame, and then write the number. Repeat using 1 more counter. What do you notice about the numbers? Do they get larger or smaller as you count?*

I can ...
count forward from any number to a number within 20.

I can also look for patterns.

Learn Glossary

| 1 | 2 | 3 | 4 | 5 | 6 | 7 | 8 | 9 | 10 |
| 11 | 12 | 13 | 14 | 15 | 16 | 17 | 18 | 19 | 20 |

Count forward.

8 9 10 11 12 13

Guided Practice

1

| 1 | 2 | 3 | 4 | 5 | 6 | 7 | 8 | 9 | 10 |
| 11 | 12 | 13 | 14 | 15 | 16 | 17 | 18 | 19 | 20 |

15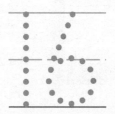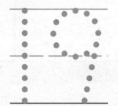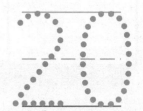

Directions Have students find the blue number on the number chart, count forward until they reach the stop sign, and then write each number they counted.

© Pearson Education, Inc. K
Topic 9 | Lesson 5

Name _____

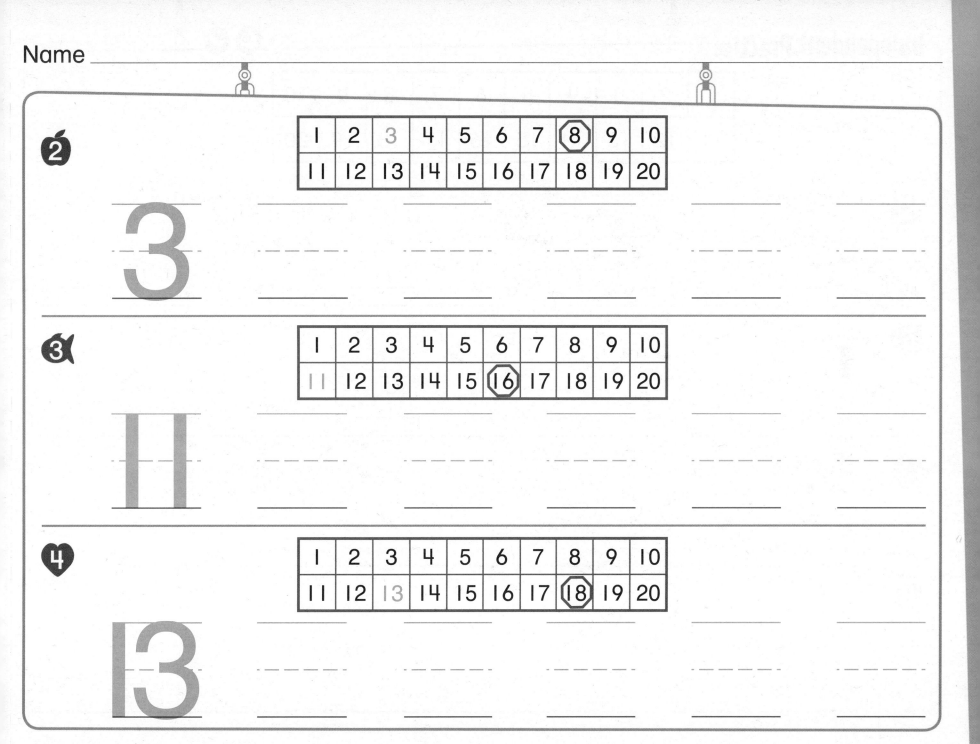

❷

1	2	3	4	5	6	7	8	9	10
11	12	13	14	15	16	17	18	19	20

3

❸

1	2	3	4	5	6	7	8	9	10
11	12	13	14	15	16	17	18	19	20

11

4

1	2	3	4	5	6	7	8	9	10
11	12	13	14	15	16	17	18	19	20

13

Directions ❷–❹ Have students find the blue number on the number chart, count forward until they reach the stop sign, and then write each number they counted.

Independent Practice

1	2	3	4	5	6	7	8	9	10
11	12	13	14	15	16	17	18	19	20

✋ **5** 7

☕ **6** 10

🌲 **7** 12

🚩 **8**

Directions ✋–🚩 Have students start at the blue number and count forward, and then write each number they counted. Have students use the number chart at the top of the page, if needed. 🚩 **Higher Order Thinking** Have students pick a number between 1 and 15, and write it on the first line. Have them count forward, and then write each number they counted.

© Pearson Education, Inc. K

Name _____

Another Look!

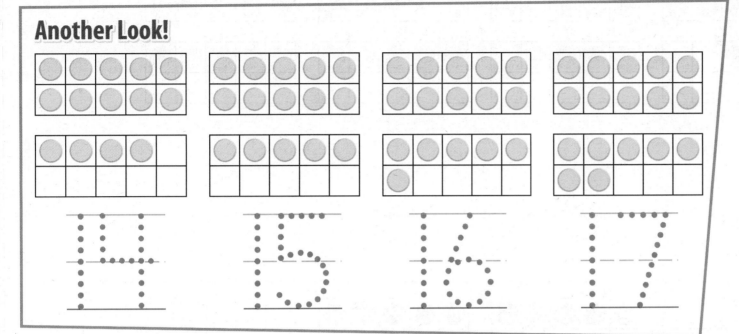

14 15 16 17

HOME ACTIVITY Pick a start number between 1 and 15. Have your child write the next four numbers. Repeat using different numbers.

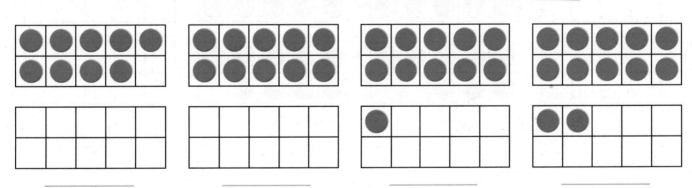

Directions Say: *The first double ten-frame shows 14 counters. The second double ten-frame shows 1 more counter. Count the counters in each double ten-frame, and then write the numbers to tell how many. Count forward to say each number you wrote.* ★ Have students count the counters in each double ten-frame, and then write the numbers to tell how many. Then have them count forward to say each number they wrote.

2

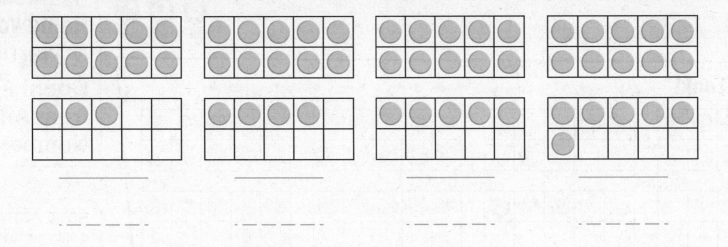

_____   _____   _____   _____

- - - - - - -   - - - - - - -   - - - - - - -   - - - - - - -

_____   _____   _____   _____

3

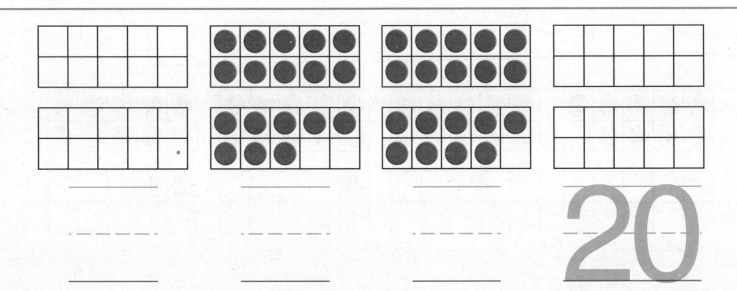

_____   _____   _____   _____

- - - - - - -   - - - - - - -   - - - - - - -   20

_____   _____   _____   _____

Directions ✌ Have students count the counters in each double ten-frame, and then write the numbers to tell how many. Then have them count forward to say each number they wrote. ✦ **Higher Order Thinking** Have students look at the counters and the number given and find the pattern. Then have them draw the missing counters in each double ten-frame, and then write the numbers to tell how many. Have students count forward to say each number they wrote.

© Pearson Education, Inc. K

Name _____

Directions Say: *Daniel has 13 cherries on a tray. Jada has 11 cherries on a tray. How can you show this? Use counters to show the cherries on the trays, and then draw the pictures. How can you tell that your drawings are correct?*

I can … count to find how many are in a group.

I can also use math tools correctly.

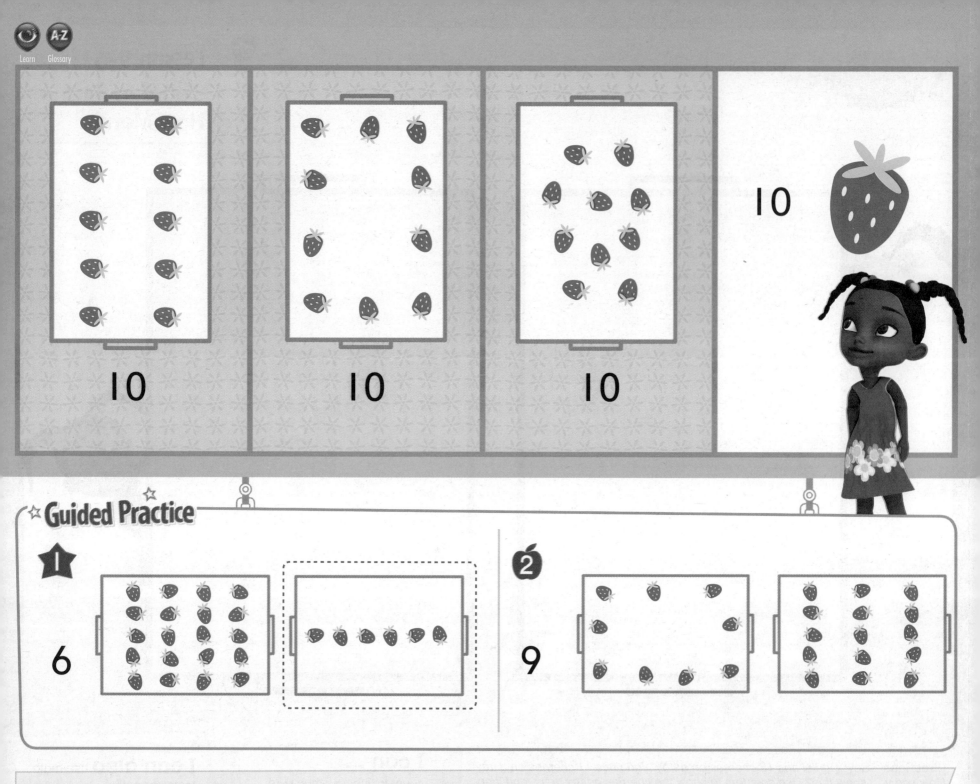

☆ **Guided Practice**

1

6

2

9

Directions Have students: **1** draw a circle around the tray with 6 strawberries; **2** draw a circle around the tray with 9 strawberries.

© Pearson Education, Inc. K

Name _____

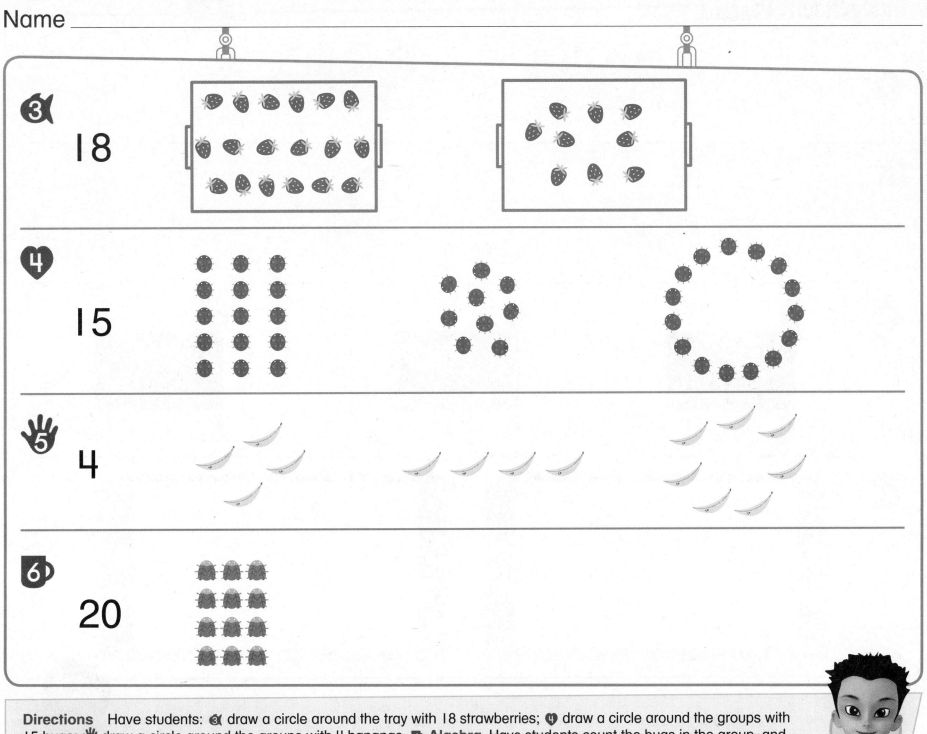

3 18

4 15

5 4

6 20

Directions Have students: **3** draw a circle around the tray with 18 strawberries; **4** draw a circle around the groups with 15 bugs; **5** draw a circle around the groups with 4 bananas. **6** **Algebra** Have students count the bugs in the group, and then draw another group of bugs so that there are 20 bugs in all.

Topic 9 | Lesson 6   five hundred forty-five **545**

Tools Assessment

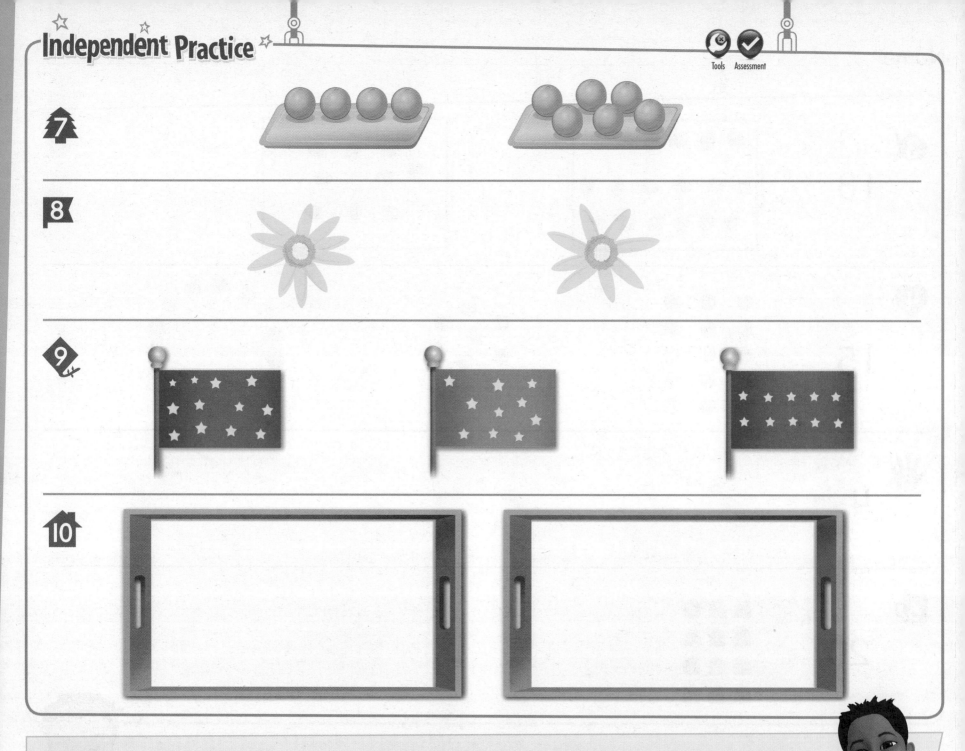

7

8

9

10

Directions Have students: **7** draw a circle around the tray with 6 oranges; **8** draw a circle around the flower with 8 petals; **9** draw a circle around the flags with 10 stars. **10** **Higher Order Thinking** Have students draw 19 strawberries in two different ways.

© Pearson Education, Inc. K

Name _____

Another Look!

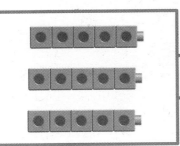

HOME ACTIVITY Give your child a handful of small items such as pennies, buttons, or dry beans. Have him or her count how many of each item there are. Count together to check your child's answers. Then line up the same number of objects in another arrangement. Have him or her count to see that the number is the same.

 1

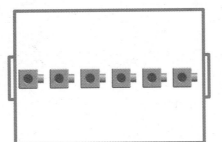

2

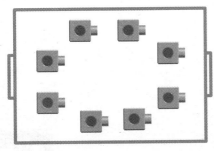

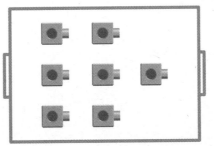

Directions Say: *Which trays have 20 connecting cubes on them? Draw a circle around the trays. How did you find how many?*
Have students: **1** draw a circle around the tray with 8 cubes; **2** draw a circle around the tray with 7 cubes.

Topic 9 | Lesson 6   Digital Resources at PearsonRealize.com   five hundred forty-seven **547**

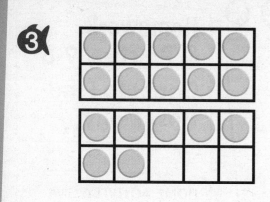 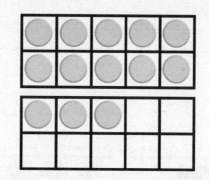 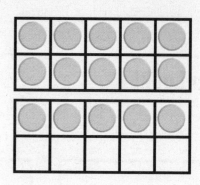

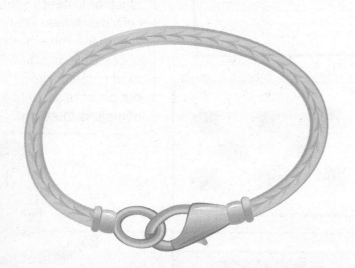

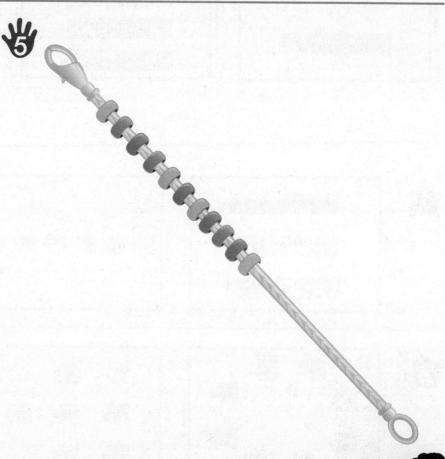

Directions ✪ Have students draw a circle around the double ten-frame with 17 counters. ♥ **Higher Order Thinking** Have students draw 11 beads on the bracelet. ✋ **Higher Order Thinking** Have students draw more beads to show 20 beads on the bracelet.

© Pearson Education, Inc. K

Topic 9 | Lesson 6

Solve

10   11   12   13   14

Directions Say: *Carlos wants to put some or all of the eggs in the carton. Draw a circle around all the numbers that tell how many eggs he could put in the carton. Explain why there could be more than one answer.*

I can ...
use reasoning to count and write numbers to the number 20.

I can also count objects in different arrangements.

Think. 10, 11, 12, 13, or 14?

I see 12.

3 possible answers

☆ Guided Practice

8   9   (10)   (11)   (12)

Directions ⭐ Say: *There are more than 8 cows on a farm. Some cows are outside the barn. 1 or more cows are inside the barn. Count the cows that are outside of the barn, and then draw a circle around the numbers that tell how many cows there could be in all.*

Topic 9 | Lesson 7

Independent Practice

 2

12   13   14   15   16

 3

16   17   18   19   20

 4

3   4   5   6   7

Directions   Say: **2** *There are more than 12 horses on the farm. Some horses are outside the stable. 0, 1, or 2 horses are inside the stable. Count the horses outside the stable, and then draw a circle around the numbers that tell how many horses there could be in all.* **3** *Some dogs are playing in the park. 1 or 2 dogs are resting in a doghouse. Count the dogs playing in the park, and then draw a circle around the numbers that tell how many dogs there could be in all.* **4** *The fish tank can hold up to 15 fish. Count the fish in the tank, and then draw a circle around the numbers that tell how many more fish could fit in the tank.*

10   11   12   13   14

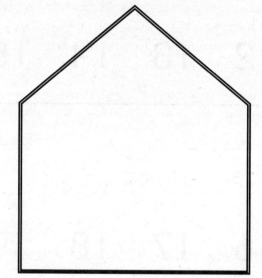

Directions Read the problem to students. Then have them use multiple problem-solving methods to solve the problem. Say: *Alex lives on a farm with so many cats that they are hard to count. Sometimes the cats are outside and sometimes they hide in the shed. Alex knows that the number of cats is greater than 11. There are less than 15 cats on the farm. How can Alex find out the number of cats that could be on his farm?* 🖐 **Reasoning** *What numbers do you know from the problem? Mark an X on the numbers that do NOT fit the clues. Draw a circle around the numbers that tell the number of cats that could be on the farm.* 6 **Model** *How can you show a word problem using pictures? Draw a picture of the cats on Alex's farm. Remember that some may hide inside the shed.* 🌲 **Explain** *Is your drawing complete? Tell a friend how your drawing shows the number of cats on Alex's farm.*

Name ______________________________

Help Tools Games

Homework & Practice 9-7
Reasoning

Another Look!

13 14 15 16 17 18

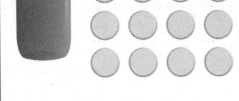

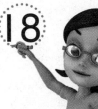

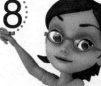

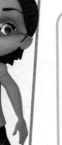

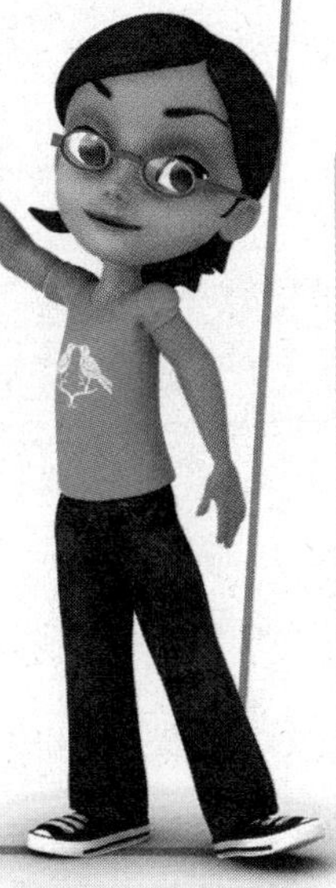

HOME ACTIVITY Put 15 coins on a table. Say: *I have some coins on the table. I am hiding 1 or more coins in my hand. How many coins could I have in all? 13, 14, 15, 16, or 17?* Have your child count the coins on the table and then explain how he or she knows how many coins there could be in all.

1

16 17 18 19 20

2

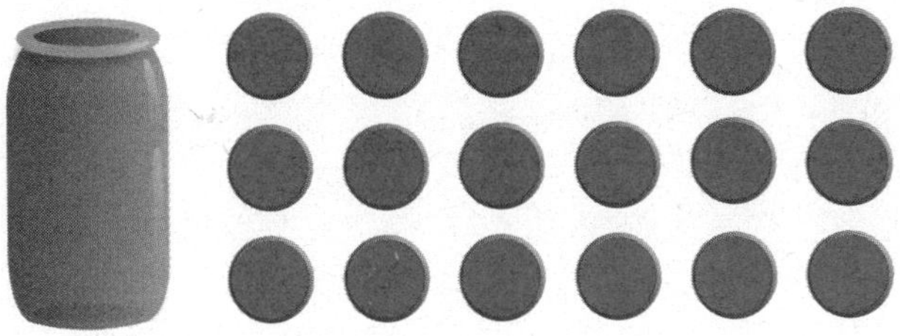

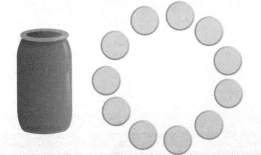

10 11 12 13 14

Directions Say: *There are 1 or more counters inside the jar. Count the yellow counters, and then draw a circle around the numbers that tell how many counters there could be in all.* 1 and 2 Say: *There are 1 or more counters inside the jar. Count the counters, and then draw a circle around the numbers that tell how many counters there could be in all.*

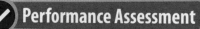

Directions Read the problem to students. Then have them use multiple problem-solving methods to solve the problem. Say: *Jada knows that there are 17 bunnies at the animal sanctuary. Some are sitting in the grass. Some are hiding behind a bush. What clues can she write to have her friends guess the number of bunnies in all?* **Make Sense** *What do you know about the problem? How many bunnies are there in all?* **Reasoning** *Tell your friend the clues. How many bunnies can he or she see?* **Explain** *If your friend says there are 14 bunnies in all, what mistake did he or she probably make?*

⭐①

2 + 3	5 – 1	2 + 2	1 + 3	4 – 0
5 – 2	0 + 4	0 + 3	2 + 1	1 + 4
2 – 1	3 + 1	5 – 1	4 + 0	1 + 3
3 + 0	2 + 2	5 – 3	5 – 4	2 + 0
1 – 1	4 – 0	2 – 0	3 + 2	1 + 0

②

_____

- - - - - - -

_____

I can …
add and subtract fluently to 5.

Directions Have students: ⭐ color each box that has a sum or difference that is equal to 4; ② write the that letter they see.

⭐ 1

13   16   18   🍎 2   **12   15   17**   🐟 3

❤️ 4

✋ 5

☕ 6

Directions   Understand Vocabulary Have students: ⭐ draw a circle around the number **sixteen**; 🍎 draw a circle around the number **twelve**; 🐟 write the number **eighteen**; ❤️ draw **eleven** counters in the box, and then write the number; ✋ draw a circle around **fourteen** cubes; ☕ write the number **twenty**.

Name _____

Set A

19

1

★ ★ ★ ★ ★ ★
★ ★ ★ ★ ★ ★
★ ★ ★ ★ ★

2

_____

Set B

1	2	3	4	5	6	7	8	9	10
11	12	13	14	15	⑯	17	18	19	20

3

1	2	3	4	5	6	7	8	9	10
⑪	12	13	14	15	16	17	18	19	20

14 15 16

9 _____

Directions Have students: **1** and **2** count the objects in each group, and then write the number to tell how many; **3** find the blue number on the number chart, count forward until they reach the stop sign, and then write each number they counted.

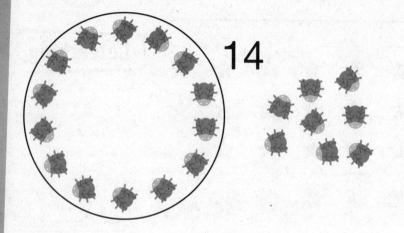

14

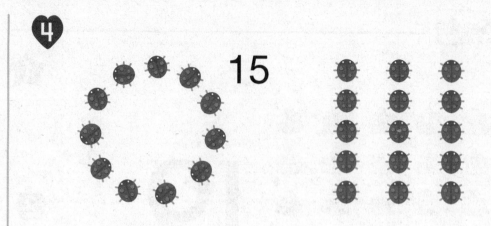

15

2   3   ④   ⑤

9   10   11   12   13

Directions Have students: ✤ draw a circle around the group with 15 bugs; ✋ listen to the story and use reasoning to find the answer. *Some bunnies are resting in the grass. 2 or 3 bunnies are playing behind the bush. Count the bunnies in the grass, and then draw a circle around the numbers that show how many bunnies there could be in all.*

Name _____

⭐ 1

(A) 13

(B) 14

(C) 15

(D) 16

🍎 2

(A)

(B)

(C)

(D)

🐟 3

14 ☐   15 ☐   16 ☐   17 ☐

Directions Have students mark the best answer. ⭐ Which number tells how many? 🍎 Which shows 11? 🐟 Have students listen to the story, and then mark all the possible answers. *There are some bees outside of the beehive. 1 or more bees are inside the beehive. Count the bees outside of the beehive, and then mark all the numbers that tell how many bees there could be in all.*

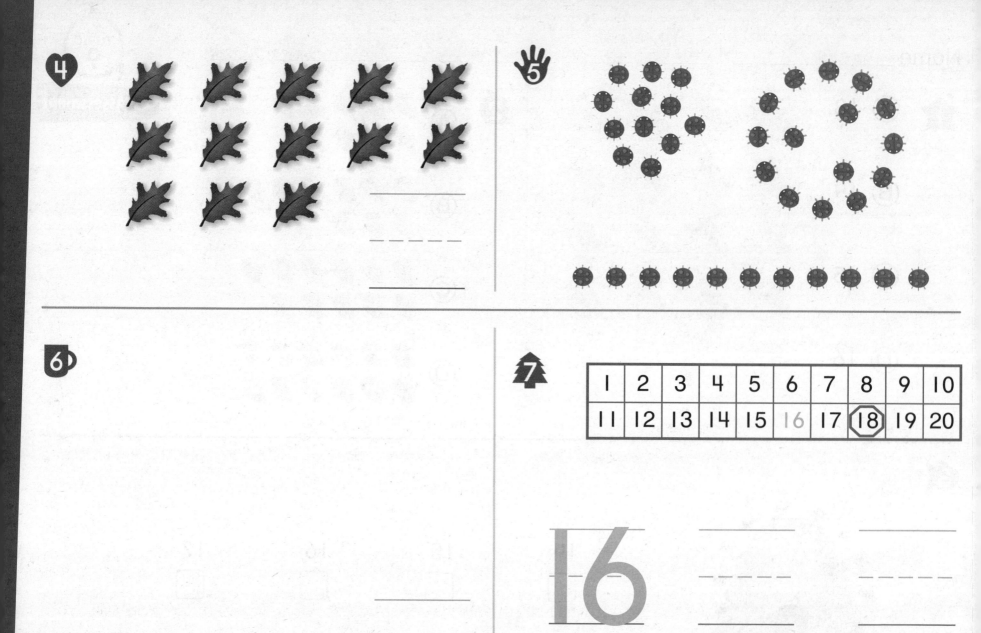

4 _____

5

6

7

1	2	3	4	5	6	7	8	9	10
11	12	13	14	15	16	17	18	19	20

16 _____ _____

Directions Have students: **4** count the leaves, and then write the number to tell how many; **5** draw a circle around the group that shows 15 ladybugs; **6** draw eighteen marbles, and then write the number to tell how many; **7** find the blue number on the number chart, count forward until they reach the stop sign, and then write each number they counted.

© Pearson Education, Inc. K

Topic 9 | Assessment

Name _____

⭐ 1

🍎 2

Directions **Sadie's Stickers** Say: *Sadie puts many stickers in her notebook. How many of each type of sticker is there?* Have students: ⭐ count the number of heart stickers, and then write the number to tell how many; 2 count the number of smiley face stickers, and then write the number to tell how many.

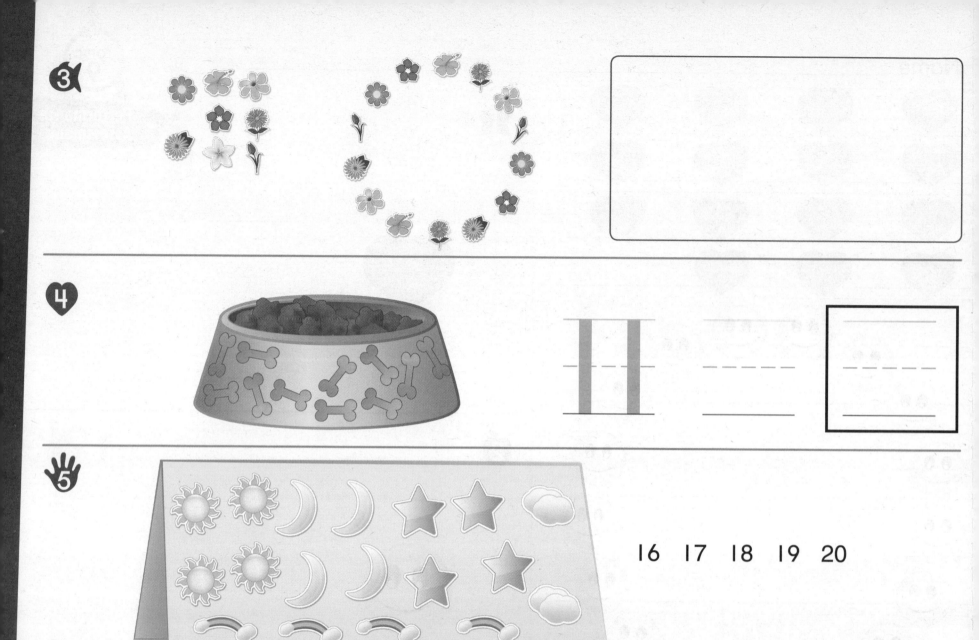

3

4

16 17 18 19 20

5

Directions ❸ Say: *Sadie wants to use 14 stickers to decorate a picture frame.* Have students draw a circle around the group of stickers that she should use, and then draw a different way to show 14 stickers. ❹ Say: *Sadie gets a sticker for feeding her dog every day. How many stickers will Sadie have in 2 days?* Have students count the stickers on the dish, count forward to find the answer, and then write each number they counted. ❺ Say: *Sadie puts some stickers on the front of a card. She puts 1 or more stickers on the back of a card.* Have students count the stickers she put on the front of the card, and then draw a circle around the numbers that show how many stickers there could be in all. Have students explain their answer.

Compose and Decompose Numbers 11 to 19

Essential Question: How can composing and decomposing numbers from 11 to 19 into ten ones and some further ones help you understand place value?

Digital Resources

Solve Learn Glossary

Tools Assessment Help Games

A desert

Sunlight causes water to evaporate faster.

Math and Science Project: Sunlight and Earth's Surface

Directions Read the character speech bubbles to students. **Find Out!** Have students find out how sunlight affects Earth's surface. Say: *Talk to friends and relatives about sunlight and how it affects Earth.* **Journal: Make a Poster** Have students make a poster that shows 3 things sunlight does for Earth. Have them draw a sun with 16 rays. Then have them write an equation for parts of 16.

Name _____

1

2

3

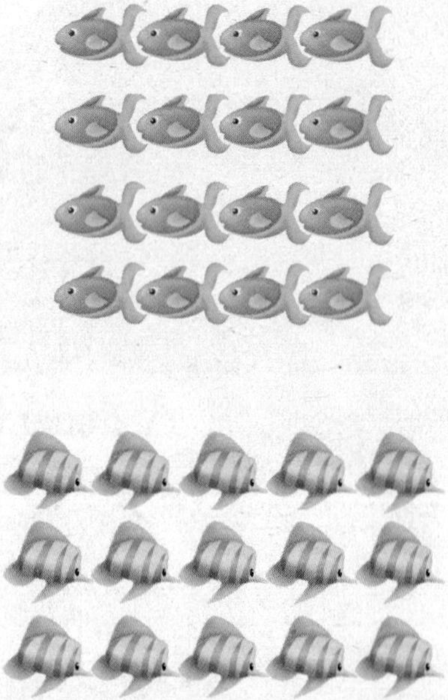

4

5

6

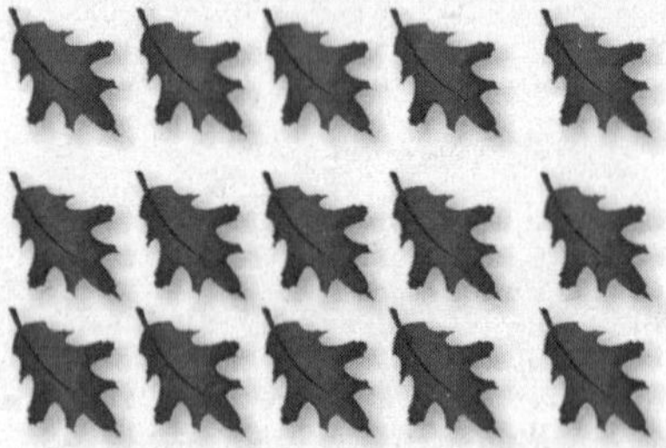

Directions Have students: **1** draw a circle around the group with 16; **2** draw a circle around the group with 20; **3** draw a circle around the group that is less than the other group; **4–6** count the leaves, and then write the number to tell how many.

© Pearson Education, Inc. K **Topic 10**

How many more?

My Word Cards

Directions Review the definitions and have students study the cards. Extend learning by having students draw pictures for each word on a separate piece of paper.

13

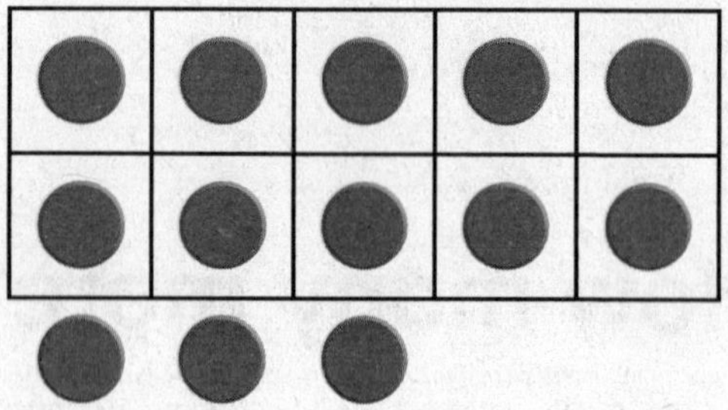

Point to the 3 counters below the ten-frame.
Say: *13 is 10 and **how many more**? 3 more.*

© Pearson Education, Inc. K

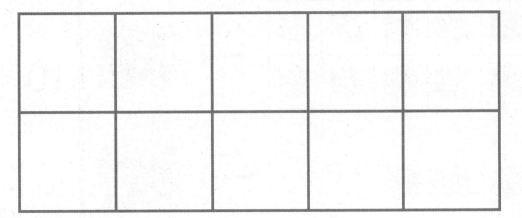

$$10 + \underline{\hspace{1.5cm}} = \underline{\hspace{1.5cm}}$$

Directions Say: *Use counters to fill the ten-frame. Put 1, 2, or 3 counters outside of the ten-frame. Draw all of the counters. What equation can you write to tell how many counters there are in all?*

I can ...
use drawings and equations to make the numbers 11, 12, and 13.

I can also model with math.

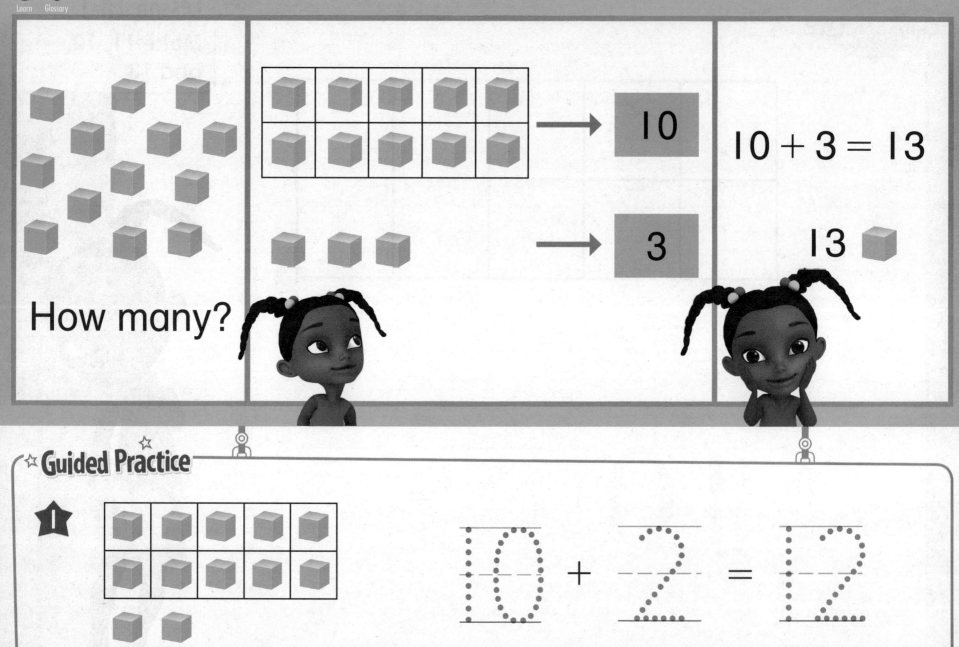

How many?

$$10 + 3 = 13$$

13

Guided Practice

1

$$10 + 2 = 12$$

Directions ⭐ Have students write an equation to match the number of blocks shown. Then have them tell how the picture and equation show 10 ones and some more ones.

Topic 10 | Lesson 1

Name _____

 2

 **3**

_____ _____ _____

- - - - - + - - - - - = - - - - -

_____ _____ _____

_____ _____ _____

- - - - - + - - - - - = - - - - -

_____ _____ _____

4

5

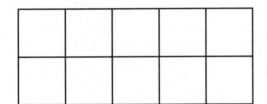

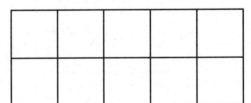

$$10 + 2 = 12$$

$$10 + 3 = 13$$

Directions Have students: **2** and **3** write an equation to match the number of blocks shown. Then have them tell how the picture and equation show 10 ones and some more ones; **4** and **5** draw blocks to match the equation. Then have them tell how the picture and equation show 10 ones and some more ones.

Independent Practice

_____ _____

- - - - + - - - - = - - - -

_____ _____

 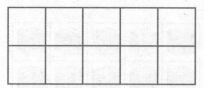

_____ _____

- - - - + - - - - = - - - -

_____ _____

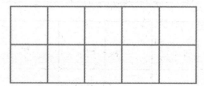

$$10 + \text{-----} = 12$$

$$13 = 10 + \text{-----}$$

Directions Have students: draw counters and write an equation to show how to make 13. Then have them tell how the picture and equation show 10 ones and some more ones; draw counters and write an equation to show how to make 11. Then have them tell how the picture and equation show 10 ones and some more ones. 🚩 **Algebra** Have students draw counters to find the missing number. Then have them tell how the picture and equation show 10 ones and some more ones. ◆ **Higher Order Thinking** Have students draw counters to find the missing number. Then have them tell how the picture and equation show 10 ones and some more ones.

Topic 10 | Lesson 1

Name _____

Another Look!

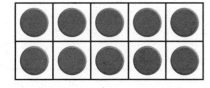
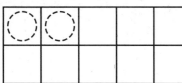

 +

HOME ACTIVITY Have your child use pennies to model and explain how to make 11, 12, and 13 with 10 ones and some more ones.

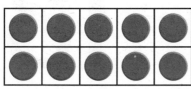

_____ _____ _____

_____ + _____ = _____

Directions Say: *You can use counters and a double ten-frame to show 12 as 10 ones and some more ones. Fill the first ten-frame with 10 counters. Then draw more counters to make 12, and write an equation to match the picture.* ⭐ Have students draw counters to make 13 and write an equation to match the picture. Then have them tell how the picture and equation show 10 ones and some more ones.

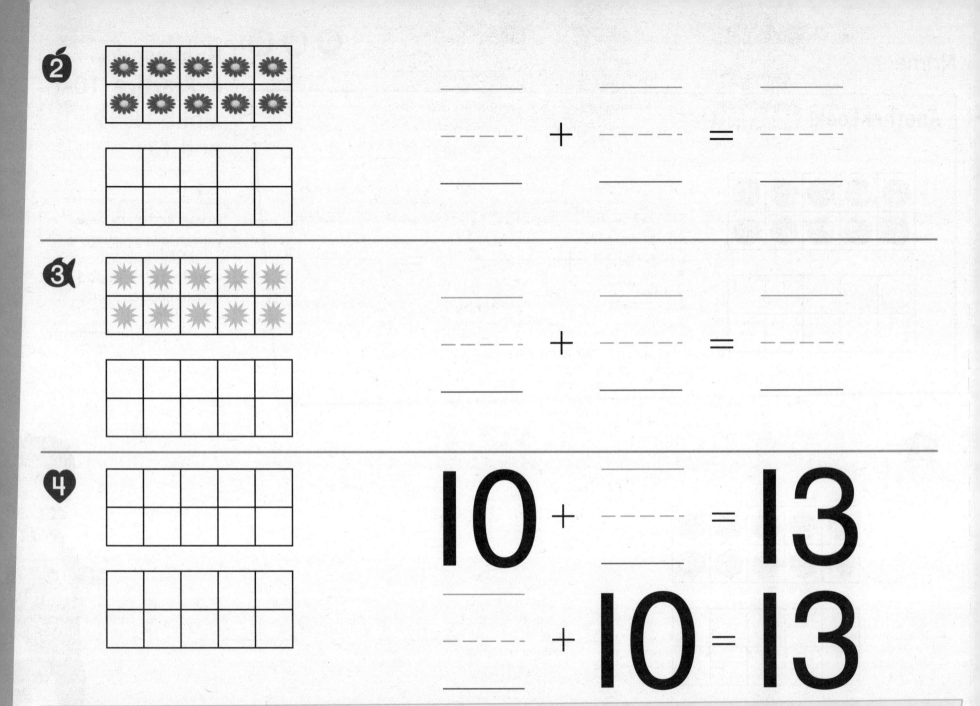

2

$$\text{---} + \text{---} = \text{---}$$

3

$$\text{---} + \text{---} = \text{---}$$

4

$$10 + \text{---} = 13$$

$$\text{---} + 10 = 13$$

© Pearson Education, Inc. K

Solve & Share

Name _____

Solve

$$ \underline{\hspace{2cm}} + \underline{\hspace{2cm}} = 15 $$

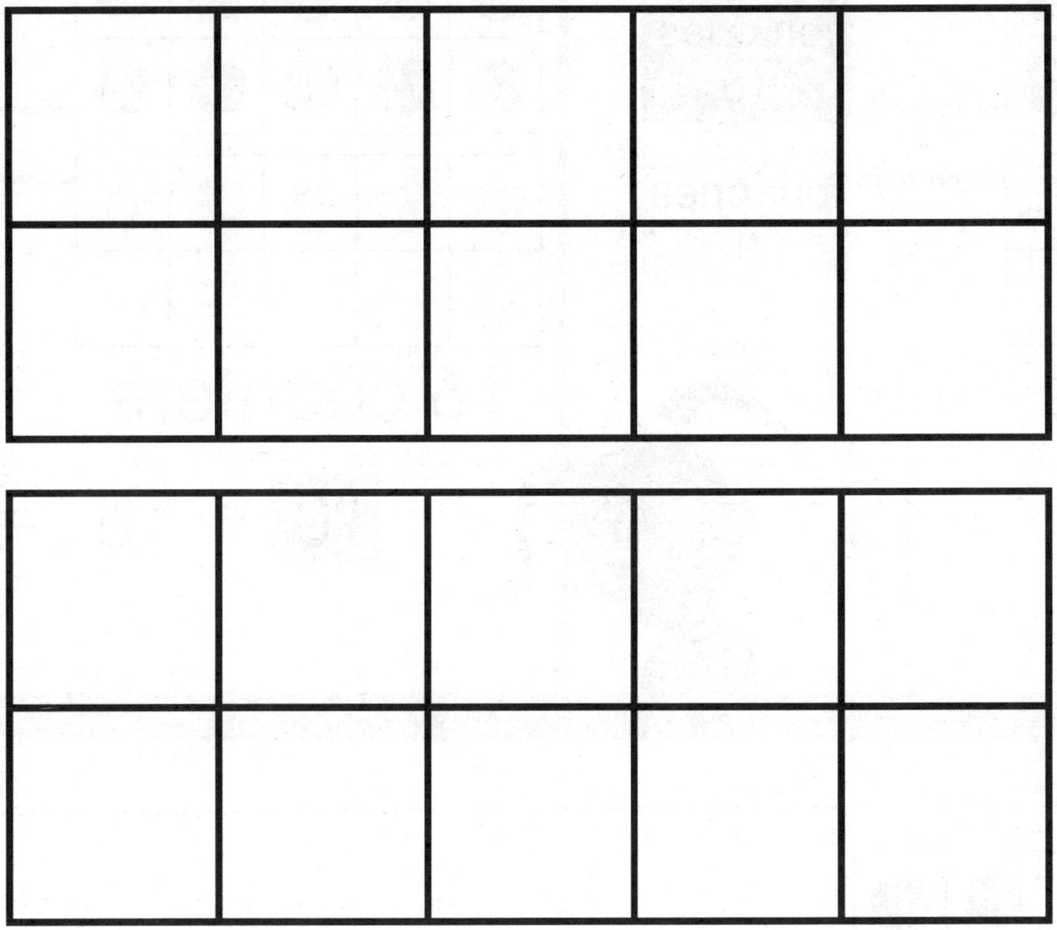

Directions Say: *Put 15 counters in the double ten-frame to show 10 ones and some more ones. Then complete the equation to match the counters.*

I can ... make the numbers 14, 15, and 16.

I can also break apart problems.

14 counters

10 + 4 = 14

16 counters

10 + 6 = 16

☆ Guided Practice

1

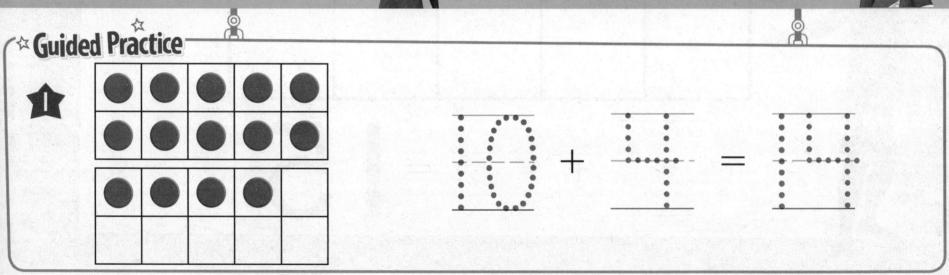

10 + 4 = 14

Directions ★ Have students write an equation to match the counters. Then have them tell how the picture and equation show 10 ones and some more ones.

© Pearson Education, Inc. K

Topic 10 | Lesson 2

Name

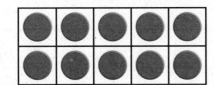

_____ + _____ = _____

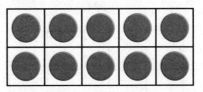

_____ + _____ = _____

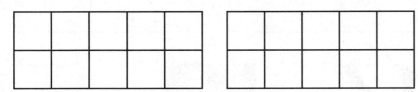

$10 + 4 = 14$

$10 + 5 = 15$

Directions Have students: 2–3 write an equation to match the counters. Then have them tell how the picture and equation show 10 ones and some more ones; 4–5 draw counters to match the equation. Then have them tell how the picture and equation show 10 ones and some more ones.

Topic 10 | Lesson 2

five hundred seventy-five **575**

Tools Assessment

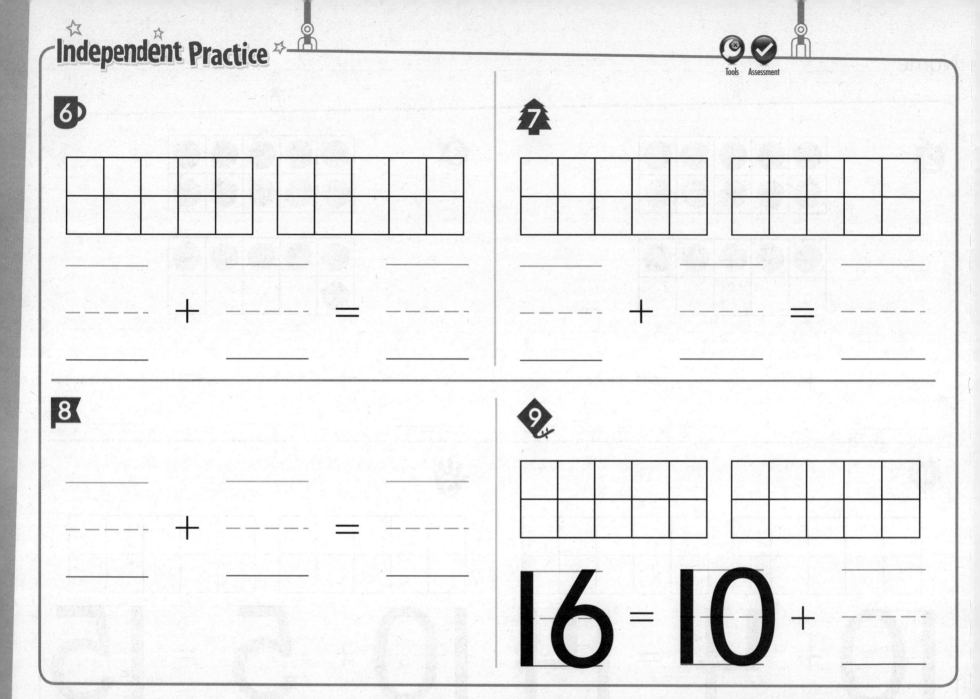

6

_____ + _____ = _____

7

_____ + _____ = _____

8

_____ + _____ = _____

9

16 = 10 + _____

Directions Have students: **6** draw counters and write an equation to show how to make 16. Then have them tell how the picture and equation show 10 ones and some more ones; **7** draw counters and write an equation to show how to make 14. Then have them tell how the picture and equation show 10 ones and some more ones. **8** **Number Sense** Have students write an equation to show 15 as 10 ones and some more ones. **9** **Higher Order Thinking** Have students draw counters to find the missing number in the equation. Then have them tell how the picture and equation show 10 ones and some more ones.

Name _____

Another Look!

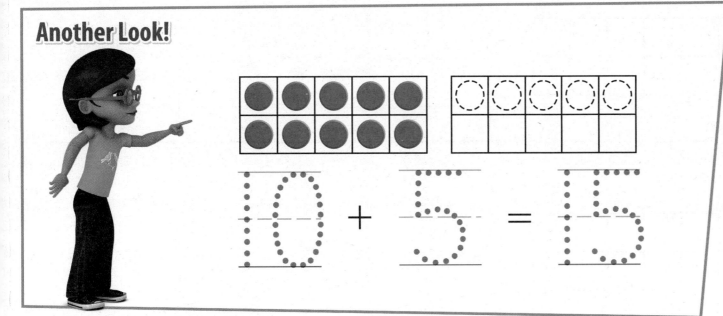

HOME ACTIVITY Have your child model the number 14 by drawing a big circle with 10 Xs inside the circle and 4 Xs outside the circle. Repeat with the numbers 15 and 16.

 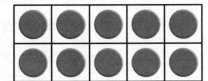 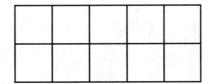  + _____ = _____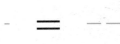

 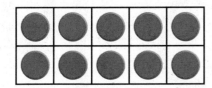 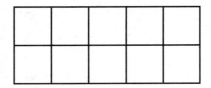 _____ + _____ = _____

Directions Say: *Finish drawing counters in the ten-frame to make 15. Then write an equation to match the picture. The picture and equation show one way to make 15 with 10 ones and some more ones.* Have students: ⭐ draw counters to make 14, and write an equation to match the picture. Then have them tell how the picture and equation show 10 ones and some more ones; 🍎 draw counters to make 16 and write an equation to match the picture. Then have them tell how the picture and equation show 10 ones and some more ones.

3

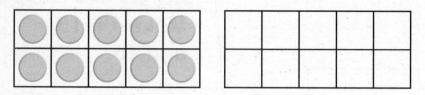

_____ + _____ = _____

4

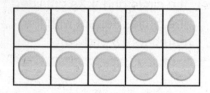 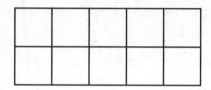

_____ + _____ = _____

5

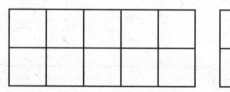 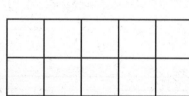

10 + _____ = 14

_____ + 10 = 14

Solve & Share

+ _____ = _____

Directions Say: *Jada made 10 prizes for the school carnival. She makes 8 more. Use counters to show how many prizes Jada made in all. Then write an equation to match the counters, and tell how the counters and equation show 10 ones and some more ones.*

I can ... make the numbers 17, 18, and 19.

I can also model with math.

$10 + 7 = 17$

$10 + 8 = 18$

$10 + 9 = 19$

$10 + 7 = 17$
$10 + 8 = 18$
$10 + 9 = 19$

↓   ↓
ten   ones
              ↓
              sum

☆ Guided Practice

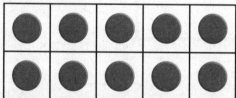

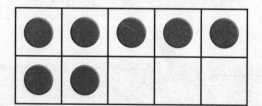

$10 + 7 = 17$

Directions ✦ Have students complete the equation to match the counters. Then have them tell how the picture and equation show 10 ones and some more ones.

Topic 10 | Lesson 3

2

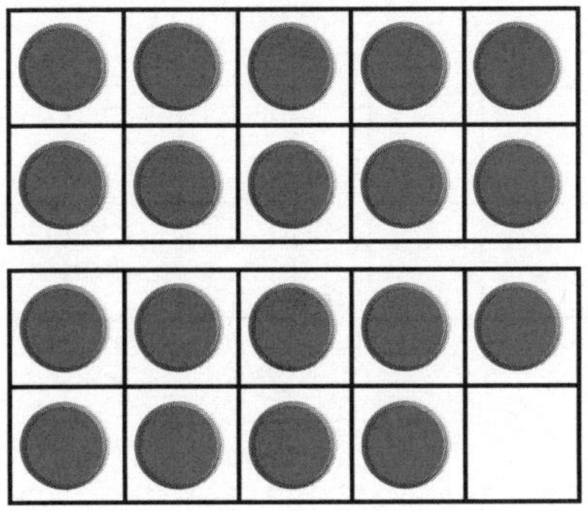

_ _ _ _ _ _ _ _ + _ _ _ _ _ _ _ = _ _ _ _ _ _ _

_ _ _ _ _ _ _

3

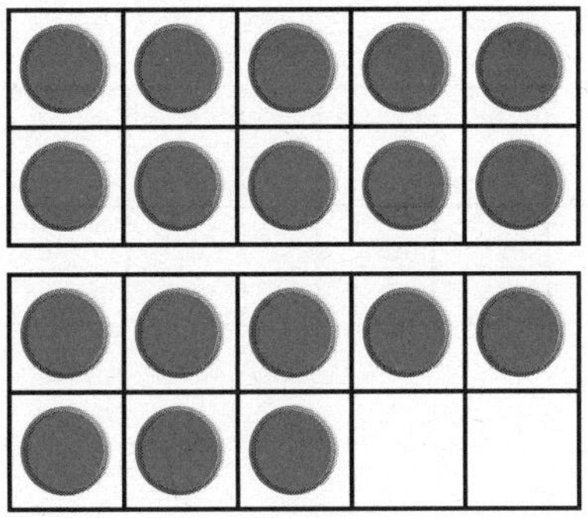

_ _ _ _ _ _ _ _ + _ _ _ _ _ _ _ = _ _ _ _ _ _ _

_ _ _ _ _ _ _

4

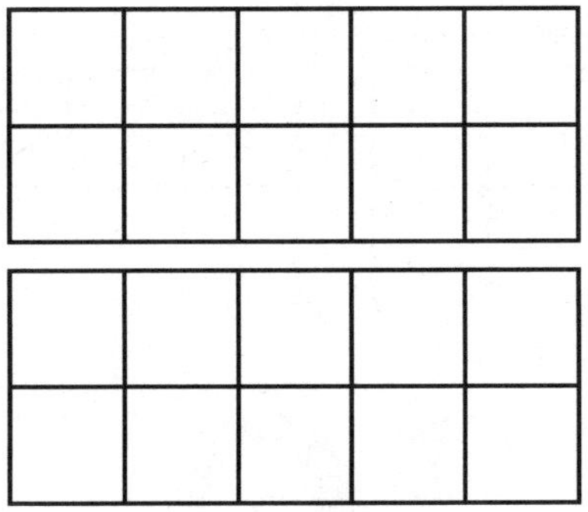

5

10 + 7 = 17   10 + 9 = 19

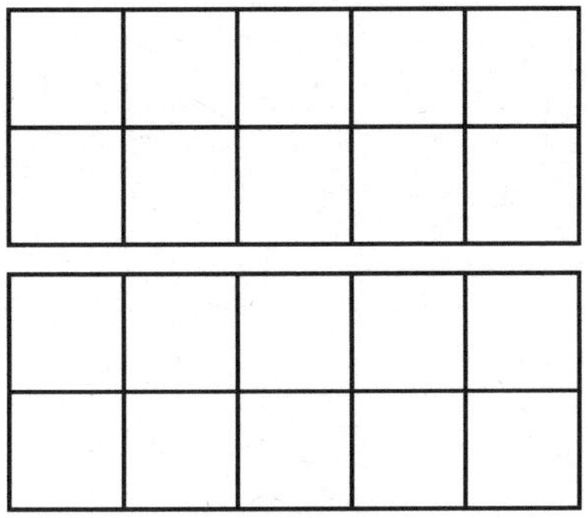

Directions Have students: **2** and **3** write an equation to match the counters. Then have them tell how the picture and equation show 10 ones and some more ones; **4** and **5** draw counters to match the equation. Then have them tell how the picture and equation show 10 ones and some more ones.

Independent Practice

6

_____ + _____ = _____

7

_____ + _____ = _____

8

_____ + _____ = _____

9

$19 = 10 +$ _____

Directions Have students: **6** draw counters, and then write an equation to show how to make 18. Then have them tell how the picture and equation show 10 ones and some more ones; **7** draw counters, and then write an equation to show how to make 19. Then have them tell how the picture and equation show 10 ones and some more ones; **8** draw counters, and then write an equation to show how to make 17. Then have them tell how the picture and equation show 10 ones and some more ones. **9 Higher Order Thinking** Have students draw counters to find the missing number in the equation. Then have them tell how the picture and equation show 10 ones and some more ones.

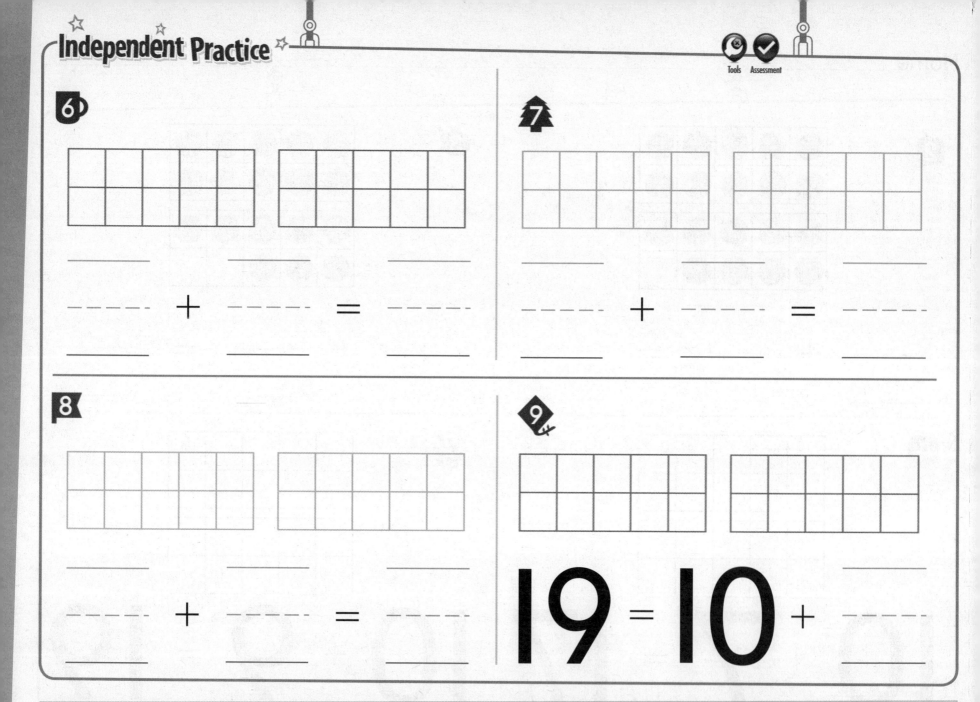

Name _____

Another Look!

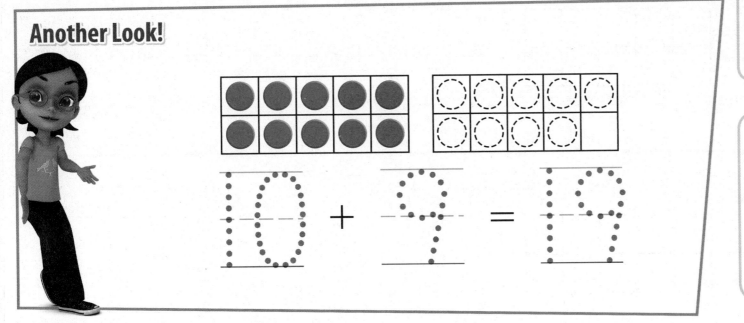

HOME ACTIVITY Place 10 marbles or other small objects in a bowl. In a second bowl, have your child count on from 10 while adding objects until there are 17 objects in all. Repeat with 19 and then 18 objects in all.

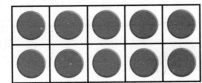 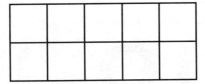 

$$\_\_\_ + \_\_\_ = \_\_\_$$

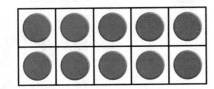 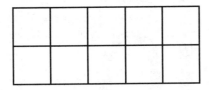

$$\_\_\_ + \_\_\_ = \_\_\_$$

Directions Say: *Finish drawing counters in the ten-frame to show how to make 19. Then write an equation to match the picture. The picture and equation show how to make 19 with 10 ones and some more ones.* Have students: ⭐ draw counters, and then write the equation to show how to make 17. Then have them tell how the picture and equation show 10 ones and some more ones; 🍎 draw counters to show how to make 18, and then write an equation to match the picture. Then have them tell how the picture and equation show 10 ones and some more ones.

3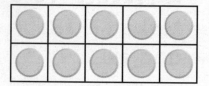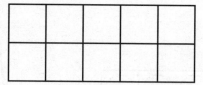

_ _ _ _ _ _ _   +   _ _ _ _ _ _ _   =   _ _ _ _ _ _ _

_ _ _ _ _ _ _   _ _ _ _ _ _ _   _ _ _ _ _ _ _

4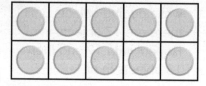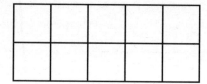

_ _ _ _ _ _ _   +   _ _ _ _ _ _ _   =   _ _ _ _ _ _ _

_ _ _ _ _ _ _   _ _ _ _ _ _ _   _ _ _ _ _ _ _

5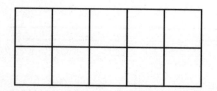

$$18 = 10 + \underline{\quad\quad}$$

$$10 + \underline{\quad\quad} = 18$$

Directions Have students: **3** draw counters to make 19, and then write an equation to match the picture. Then have them tell how the picture and equation show 10 ones and some more ones; **4** draw counters to make 17, and then write an equation to match the picture. Then have them tell how the picture and equation show 10 ones and some more ones. **5 Higher Order Thinking** Have students draw counters to find the missing numbers in the equations. Then have them tell how the picture and equation show 10 ones and some more ones.

© Pearson Education, Inc. K

Solve & Share

13 = ___ ___ + ___ ___
___ ___ ___ ___

Directions Say: *13 students wait for the train. There are only 10 seats in each train car. How many students will have to ride in a second car? Use counters to show your work. Then tell how the counters and equation show 10 ones and some more ones.*

I can ... find parts of the numbers 11, 12, and 13.

I can also break apart problems.

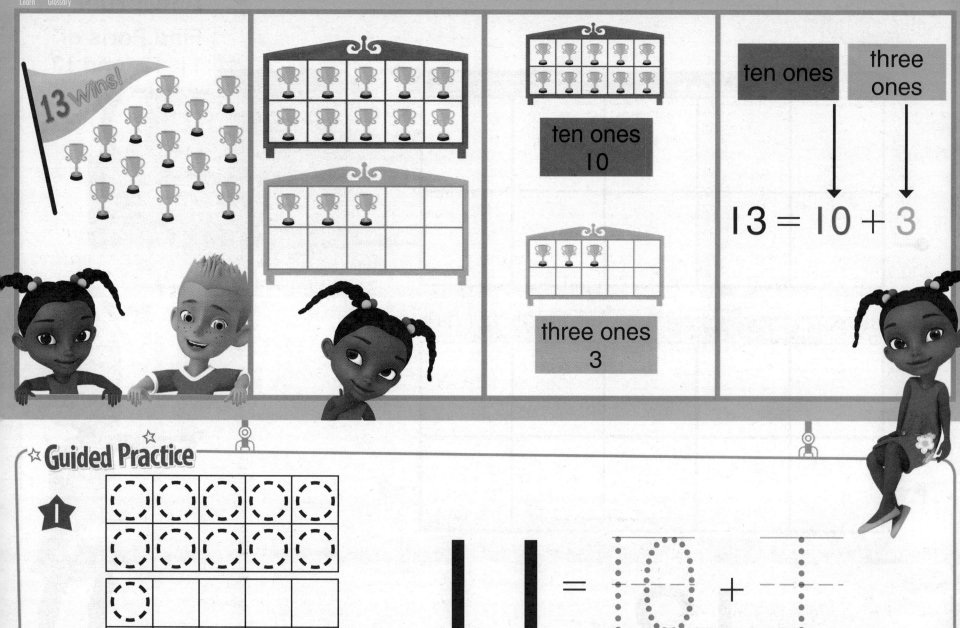

13 Wins!

ten ones
10

three ones
3

ten ones   three ones

$13 = 10 + 3$

☆ Guided Practice

⭐ 1

$||=|0|+|$

Directions ⭐ Have students use counters to show 11, draw them in the double ten-frame, and complete the equation to match the picture. Then have them tell how the picture and equation show 10 ones and some more ones.

© Pearson Education, Inc. K

Name _____

 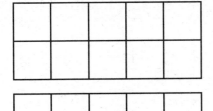

$$13 = \underline{\hspace{2cm}} + \underline{\hspace{2cm}}$$

$$12 = \underline{\hspace{2cm}} + \underline{\hspace{2cm}}$$

 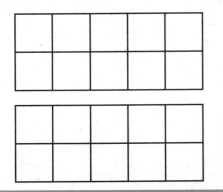

$$11 = 10 + 1$$

Directions Have students: ② use counters to show 13, draw them in the double ten-frame, and complete the equation to match the picture. Then have them tell how the picture and equation show 10 ones and some more ones; ③ use counters to show 12, draw them in the double ten-frame, and complete the equation to match the picture. Then have them tell how the picture and equation show 10 ones and some more ones; ④ draw counters to match the equation. Then have them tell how the picture and equation show 10 ones and some more ones.

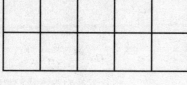

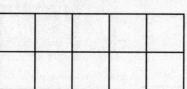

$$12 = \text{\_\_\_\_} + \text{\_\_\_\_}$$

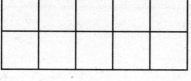

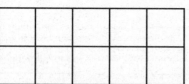

$$13 = \text{\_\_\_\_} + \text{\_\_\_\_}$$

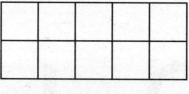

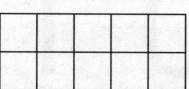

$$\text{\_\_\_\_} = \text{\_\_\_\_} + \text{\_\_\_\_}$$

$$\text{\_\_\_\_} + \text{\_\_\_\_} = \text{\_\_\_\_}$$

Directions Have students: draw counters to make 12, and complete the equation to match the picture. Then have them tell how the picture and equation show 10 ones and some more ones; draw counters to make 13, and complete the equation to match the picture. Then have them tell how the picture and equation show 10 ones and some more ones. **Higher Order Thinking** Have students draw counters to show 11 and write two equations to match the picture. Then have them tell how the picture and equations show 10 ones and some more ones.

Topic 10 | Lesson 4

Name _____

Another Look!

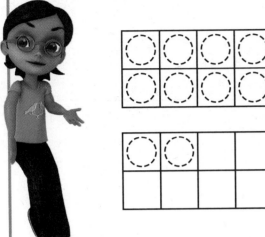

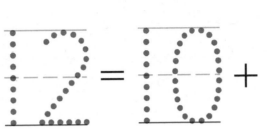

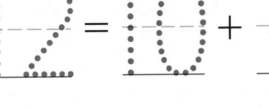

$12 = 10 + 2$

HOME ACTIVITY Have your child sort a group of 12 pencils into one group of 10 pencils and one group of 2 pencils. Discuss how many pencils are in each group and how many pencils there are in all. Repeat with 13 pencils and 11 pencils.

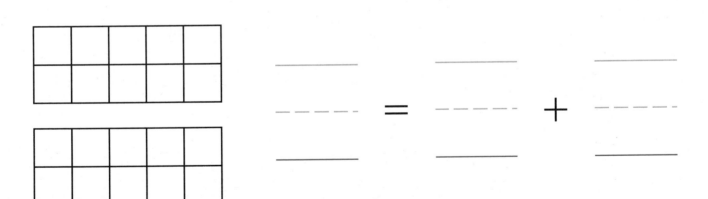

_____ = _____ + _____

Directions Say: *Draw counters in the double ten-frame to show 12 and write an equation to match the picture. The picture and equation show 10 ones and some more ones.* ⭐ Have students draw counters to show 11 and write an equation to match the picture. Then have them tell how the picture and equation show 10 ones and some more ones.

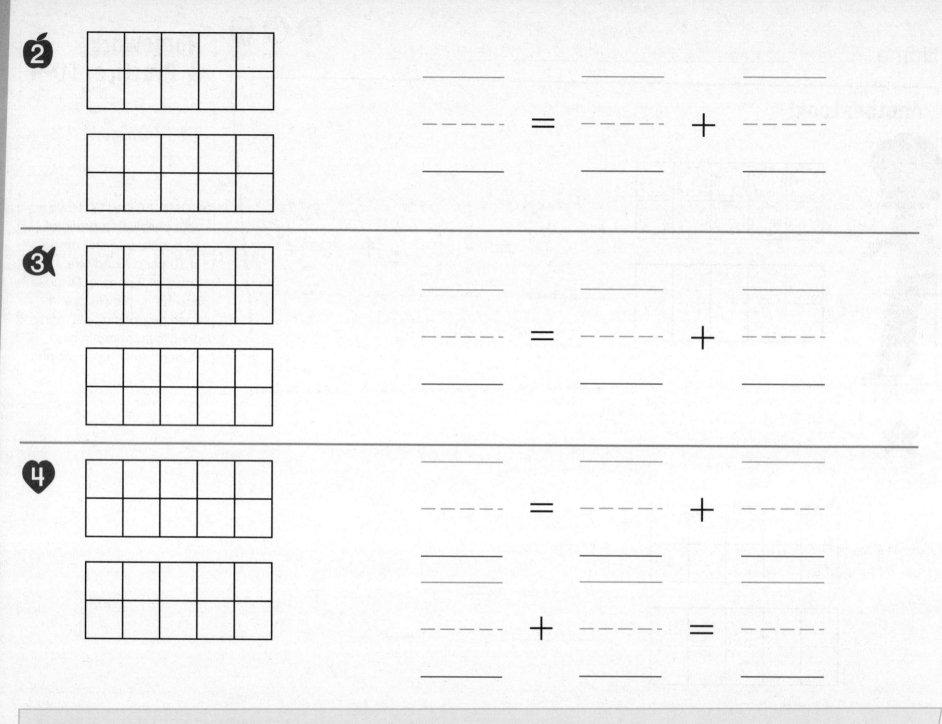

2 ____ = ____ + ____

3 ____ = ____ + ____

4 ____ = ____ + ____

____ + ____ = ____

Directions Have students: **2** draw counters to show 13 and write an equation to match the picture. Then have them tell how the picture and equation show 10 ones and some more ones; **3** draw counters to show 12 and write an equation to match the picture. Then have them tell how the picture and equation show 10 ones and some more ones. **4 Higher Order Thinking** Have students draw counters to show 13 and write two equations to match the picture. Then have them tell how the picture and equation show 10 ones and some more ones.

© Pearson Education, Inc. K

Solve & Share

Name _____

$$14 = \text{\_\_\_\_\_} + \text{\_\_\_\_\_}$$

Directions Say: 14 students go to the zoo. The first bus takes 10 students. The rest of the students go on a second bus. Use counters to describe this situation. Then complete the equation to match the counters and tell how the counters and equation show 10 ones and some more ones.

I can ... find parts of the numbers 14, 15, and 16.

I can also break apart problems.

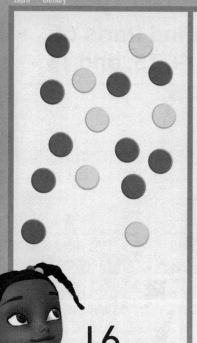

16

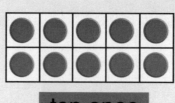
ten ones
10

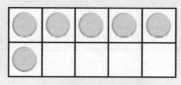
six ones
6

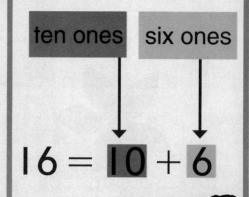
ten ones   six ones

$16 = 10 + 6$

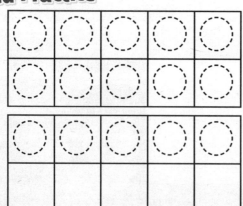

$15 = 10 + 5$

Directions  Have students use counters to show 15, draw them in the double ten-frame, and complete the equation to match the picture. Then have them tell how the picture and equation show 10 ones and some more ones.

Name _____

 2

$14 =$  _____ + _____

3

$16 =$ _____ + _____

4

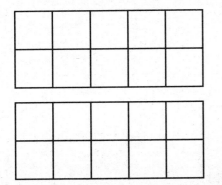

$15 = 10 + 5$

Directions Have students: **2** use counters to show 14, draw them in the double ten-frame, and complete the equation to match the picture. Then have them tell how the picture and equation show 10 ones and some more ones; **3** use counters to show 16, draw them in the double ten-frame, and complete the equation to match the picture. Then have them tell how the picture and equation show 10 ones and some more ones; **4** draw counters to match the equation. Then have them tell how the picture and equation show 10 ones and some more ones.

Independent Practice

 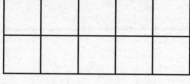

$$16 = 10 + 6$$

 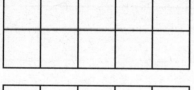

$$14 = 10 + 4$$

_____ = _____ + _____

_____   _____   _____

_____ + _____ = _____

Directions and Have students draw counters to match the equation. Then have them tell how the picture and equation show 10 ones and some more ones. 🌲 **Higher Order Thinking** Have students use counters to show 16, draw them in the double ten-frame, and complete two equations to match the picture. Then have them tell how the picture and equations show 10 ones and some more ones.

   Topic 10 | Lesson 5

Name _____

Another Look!

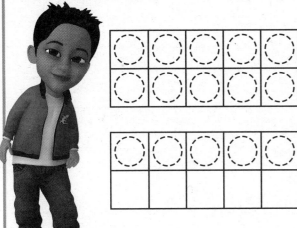

$$15 = 10 + 5$$

HOME ACTIVITY Draw 14 boxes, and then shade 10 of them. Have your child tell how many boxes there are in all. Then have your child tell how many boxes are shaded and how many boxes are NOT shaded. Repeat with 16 boxes and 15 boxes.

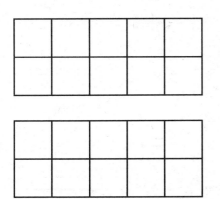

$$14 = \underline{\quad\quad} + \underline{\quad\quad}$$

Directions Say: *Draw counters in the double ten-frame to show 15 and complete the equation to match the picture. The picture and equation show 10 ones and some more ones.* ⭐ Have students draw counters to show 14 and complete the equation to match the picture. Then have them tell how the picture and equation show 10 ones and some more ones.

2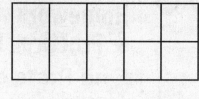

$16 =$ _____ $+$ _____

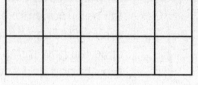

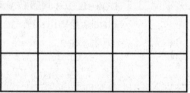

$15 =$ _____ $+$ _____

4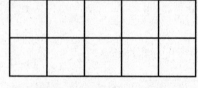

_____ $=$ _____ $+$ _____

_____ $+$ _____ $=$ _____

Directions Have students: **2** draw counters to show 16 and complete the equation to match the picture. Then have them tell how the picture and equation show 10 ones and some more ones; **3** draw counters to show 15 and complete the equation to match the picture. Then have them tell how the picture and equation show 10 ones and some more ones. **4** **Higher Order Thinking** Have students draw counters to show 14 and write two equations to match the picture. Then have them tell how the picture and equations show 10 ones and some more ones.

© Pearson Education, Inc. K

Solve & Share

Name _____

Solve

$\boxed{} = \boxed{} + \boxed{}$

Directions Say: *How can these 18 boxes be split into ten ones and some more ones? Use 2 different color crayons to color the boxes to show your work. Then write an equation to match the picture.*

I can ...
Find parts of the numbers 17, 18, and 19.

I can also model with math.

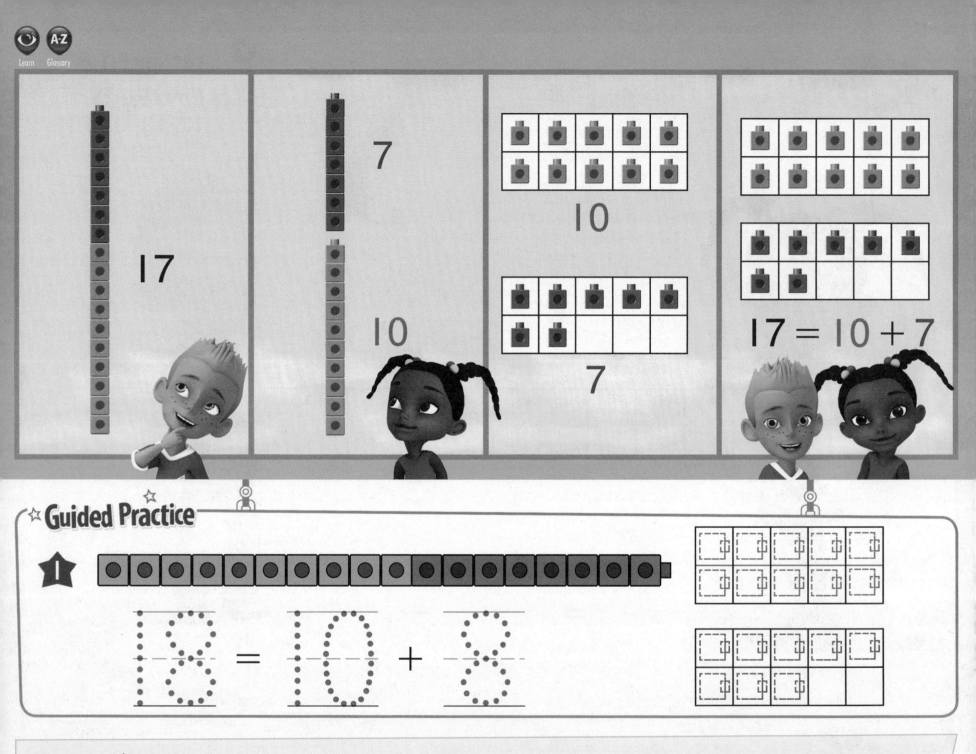

17

7
10

10

7

17 = 10 + 7

☆ **Guided Practice**

⭐1

18 = 10 + 8

Directions ⭐ Have students color 10 cubes blue to show 10 ones, and then draw 10 blue cubes in the top ten-frame. Have them color the remaining cubes in the train red to show more ones, count them, and then draw red cubes in the bottom ten-frame. Then have them write an equation to match the pictures.

© Pearson Education, Inc. K

Name _____

2

$\_\_\_\_\_$ $\_\_\_\_\_$ $\_\_\_\_\_$

$\_\_\_\_\_ = \_\_\_\_\_ + \_\_\_\_\_$

$\_\_\_\_\_$ $\_\_\_\_\_$ $\_\_\_\_\_$

3

$\_\_\_\_\_$ $\_\_\_\_\_$ $\_\_\_\_\_$

$\_\_\_\_\_ = \_\_\_\_\_ + \_\_\_\_\_$

$\_\_\_\_\_$ $\_\_\_\_\_$ $\_\_\_\_\_$

4

$18 = \_\_\_\_\_ + \_\_\_\_\_$

Directions Have students: **2** and **3** color 10 squares blue to show 10 ones, and then draw 10 blue squares in the top ten-frame. Have them color the remaining cubes in the train red to show more ones, count them, and then draw red squares in the bottom ten-frame. Then have them write an equation to match the pictures; **4** complete the equation to match the counters. Then have them tell how the picture and equation show 10 ones and some more ones.

 Independent Practice

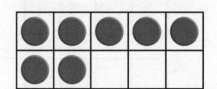

17 = _____ + _____

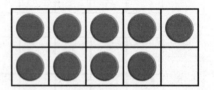

19 = _____ + _____

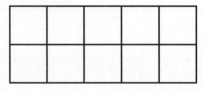

_____ = _____ + _____

_____ + _____ = _____

Directions 👋 and ☕ Have students complete the equation to match the counters. Then have them tell how the picture and equation show 10 ones and some more ones. 🌲 **Higher Order Thinking** Have students use counters to show 18, draw them in the double ten-frame, and write two equations to match the picture. Then have them tell how the picture and equations show 10 ones and some more ones.

Topic 10 | Lesson 6

Name _____

Another Look!

$$18 = 10 + 8$$

HOME ACTIVITY Have your child sort a group of 18 objects into a group of 10 and a group of 8. Discuss how many objects there are in each group and how many there are in all. Repeat with 17 objects and 19 objects.

$$17 = \underline{\hspace{1cm}} + \underline{\hspace{1cm}}$$

Directions Say: *Draw counters to show 18, and then complete the equation to match. How does the picture and equation show 10 ones and some more ones?* ⭐ Have students draw counters to show 17, and then complete the equation to match the picture. Then have them tell how the picture and equation show 10 ones and some more ones.

Topic 10 | Lesson 6   Digital Resources at PearsonRealize.com   six hundred one **601**

 **2**

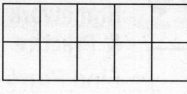

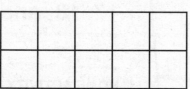

$19 =$ _____ $+$ _____

 3

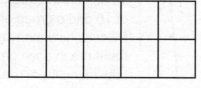

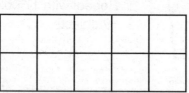

$18 =$ _____ $+$ _____

 4

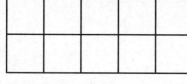

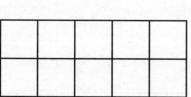

_____ $=$ _____ $+$ _____

_____ $+$ _____ $=$ _____

Directions Have students: **2** draw counters to show 19, and then complete the equation to match the picture. Then have them tell how the picture and equation show 10 ones and some more ones; **3** draw counters to show 18, and then complete the equation to match the picture. Then have them tell how the picture and equation show 10 ones and some more ones. **4 Higher Order Thinking** draw counters to show 17, and then write two equations to match the picture. Then have them tell how the picture and equations show 10 ones and some more ones.

Name _____

Solve

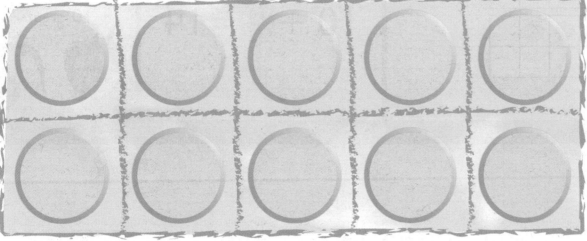

Directions Say: *Put some counters in the red five-frame. Use a red crayon and write the number that tells how many counters are in the red frame. Put the same number of counters in the blue five-frame. Use a blue crayon and write the number that tells how many counters are in the blue frames. Show the numbers to a partner. What patterns do you see?*

I can ...
use patterns to make and find the parts of numbers to 19.

I can also use addition to show my work.

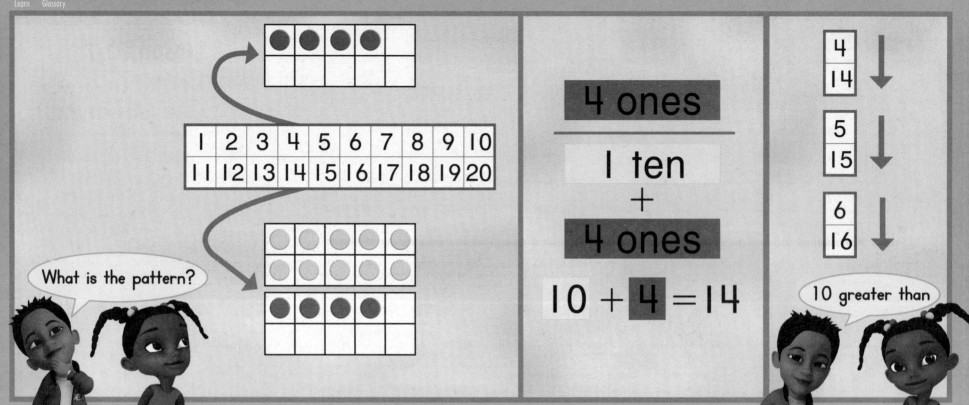

What is the pattern?

4 ones

1 ten
+
4 ones

10 + 4 = 14

10 greater than

☆ Guided Practice

1

1	2	3	4	5	6	7	8	9	10
11	12	13	14	15	16	17	18	19	20

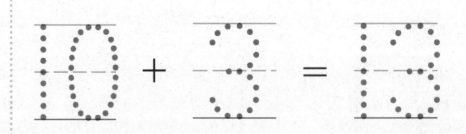

10 + 3 = 13

Directions ⭐ Have students find the number with the blue box around it, and then color the number that is 10 greater than the number in the blue box. Have them write an equation to match, and then tell how the equation shows 10 ones and some more ones. Then have students explain the pattern they made.

© Pearson Education, Inc. K   **Topic 10** | Lesson 7

Independent Practice

2

1	2	3	4	5	6	7	8	9	10
11	12	13	14	15	16	17	18	19	20

_____ + _____ = _____

3

1	2	3	4	5	6	7	8	9	10
11	12	13	14	15	16	17	18	19	20

_____ + _____ = _____

4

1	2	3	4	5	6	7	8	9	10
11	12	13	14	15	16	17	18	19	20

_____ + _____ = _____

5

$10 + 1 = 11$ $10 + 2 = 12$ _____ + _____ = **13**

Directions Have students: **2**–**4** find the number with the blue box around it, and color the number that is 10 greater than the number in the blue box. Then have them write an equation to match, and then tell how the equation shows 10 ones and some more ones; **5** complete the equation to continue the pattern, and then explain the pattern they made.

Problem Solving

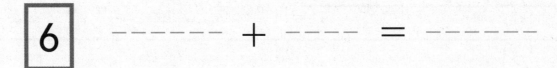

1	2	3	4	5	6	7	8	9	10
11	12	13	14	15	16	17	18	19	20

6   _____ + _____ = _____

7   _____ + _____ = _____

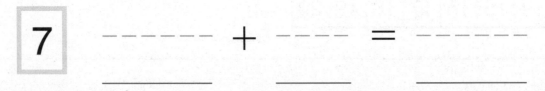

Directions Read the problem to students. Then have them use multiple problem-solving methods to solve the problem. Say: *Mr. Shepard's class will exchange cards at a holiday party. There are 16 students in the class. The store sells cards in packs of 10. Alex already has 6 cards. Marta already has 7 cards. How many cards will Alex and Marta have after they each buy one pack of cards?* 🥤 **Use Structure** *How can the number chart help you solve the problem? Write the equations for the number of cards Alex and Marta will have.* 🎄 **Generalize** *After you find the number of cards Alex will have, is it easier to find the number of cards Marta will have?* 🚩 **Explain** *Tell a friend why your answers are correct. Then tell the friend about the patterns you see in the number chart and how the equations show 10 ones and some more ones.*

© Pearson Education, Inc. K

Name _____

Another Look!

| 9 | |

| 19 | |

$$10 + 9 = 19$$

HOME ACTIVITY Take 11 pennies or other small household objects and arrange them in the following manner: two rows of 5 pennies, and a single penny underneath. Have your child write the equation that describes the number of pennies ($10 + 1 = 11$). Repeat for quantities of 12 pennies, 13 pennies, and so on, up to 19 pennies. Have your child explain the pattern in the equations that he or she has written.

| 6 | 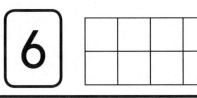 |

| 16 | 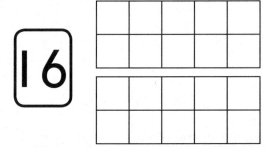 |

_____ + _____ = _____

Directions Say: *Read the numbers on the cards, and then draw counters in the top ten-frame to show 9 and in the bottom ten-frames to show 19. Write an equation to match the drawings in the ten-frames. Tell how the picture and the equation show 10 ones and some more ones.* ⭐ Have students read the numbers on the cards, and then draw counters in both the top and bottom ten-frames to show how many. Then have them write an equation to match the drawings in the ten-frames. Have students tell how the picture and the equation show 10 ones and some more ones.

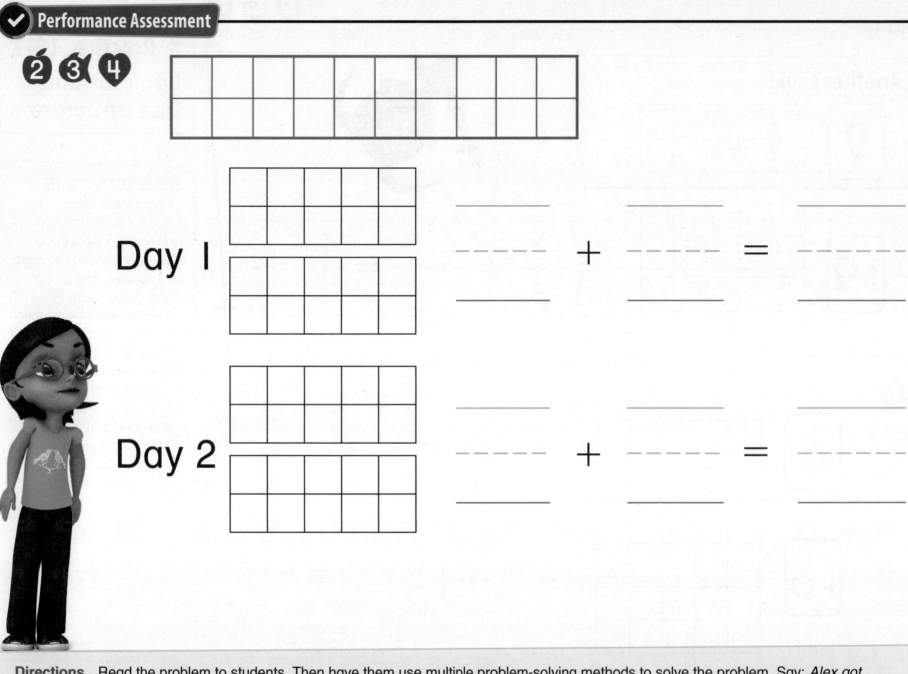

Day 1

_____ + _____ = _____

Day 2

_____ + _____ = _____

Directions Read the problem to students. Then have them use multiple problem-solving methods to solve the problem. Say: *Alex got a new tablet computer. It came loaded with 10 apps. Every day, Alex is allowed to upload 1 more app. How many apps will Alex have in two days?* ② **Model** *Can a model help you solve the problem? Write the numbers in the number chart. Which numbers will help solve this problem?* ③ **Use Tools** *How can you use the ten-frames to help? Draw counters to show how many apps there will be on Alex's tablet for each day. Then write equations to help you see the pattern.* ④ **Use Structure** *How many apps will Alex have in three days? How did seeing a pattern help you solve the problem? Explain your answer.*

© Pearson Education, Inc. K

⭐ 1

O	G	D
2 + 3	4 − 2	5 − 2

② 2

W	C	O
2 − 1	2 + 2	1 − 1

4 − 1	4 + 1	1 + 1

1 + 3	0 + 0	5 − 4

Directions ⭐ and ② Have students find a partner. Have them point to a clue in the top row, and then solve the addition or subtraction problem. Then have them look at the clues in the bottom row to find a match, and then write the clue letter above the match. Have students find a match for every clue.

I can ...
add and subtract fluently within 5.

$$10 + \underline{} = 15$$

$$19 = 10 + \underline{}$$

Directions **Understand Vocabulary** Have students: ★ complete the drawing and the equation to show **how many more** counters are needed to make 15; ✿ complete the drawing and the equation to show **how many more** counters are needed to make 19.

Name _____

Set A _____

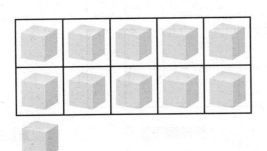

$$10 + 1 = 11$$

 ★ 1

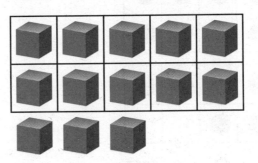

_____   + _____ = _____

_____   _____

Set B _____

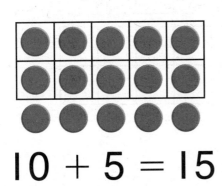

$$10 + 5 = 15$$

2

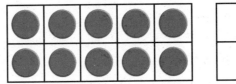 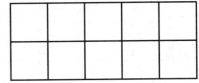

_____   + _____ = _____

_____   _____

Directions Have students: ★ write an equation to match the blocks. Then have them tell how the picture and equation show 10 ones and some more ones; 2 draw counters to show 16, and then write an equation to match the picture. Then tell how the picture and equation show 10 ones and some more ones.

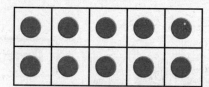

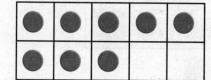

$$10 + 8 = 18$$

❸

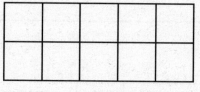

$$10 + 7 = 17$$

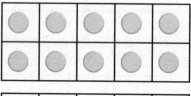

$$12 = 10 + 2$$

♥

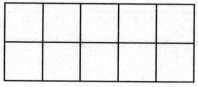

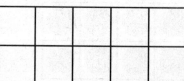

$$11 = \underline{\quad} + \underline{\quad}$$

Directions Have students: ❸ draw counters to match the equation. Then have them tell how the picture and equation show 10 ones and some more ones; ❹ draw counters to make 11, and then complete the equation to match the picture. Then have them tell how the picture and equation show 10 ones and some more ones.

Name _____

_____

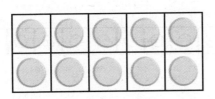

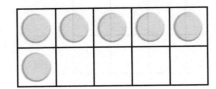

$$16 = 10 + 6$$

✋ 5

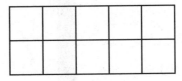

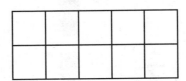

$$14 = \underline{\hspace{3cm}} + \underline{\hspace{3cm}}$$

Set F _____

1	2	3	4	5	6	7	8	9	10
11	12	13	14	15	16	17	18	19	20

$$19 = 10 + 9$$

6

1	2	3	4	5	6	7	8	9	10
11	12	13	14	15	16	17	18	19	20

$$\underline{\hspace{3cm}} + \underline{\hspace{3cm}} = \underline{\hspace{3cm}}$$

Directions Have students: ✋ use counters to show 14, draw them in the double ten-frame, and complete the equation to match the picture. Then have them tell how the picture and equation show 10 ones and some more ones; 6 find the number with the blue box around it, and color the number that is 10 greater than the number in the blue box. Then have them write an equation to match, and then tell how the equation shows 10 ones and some more ones.

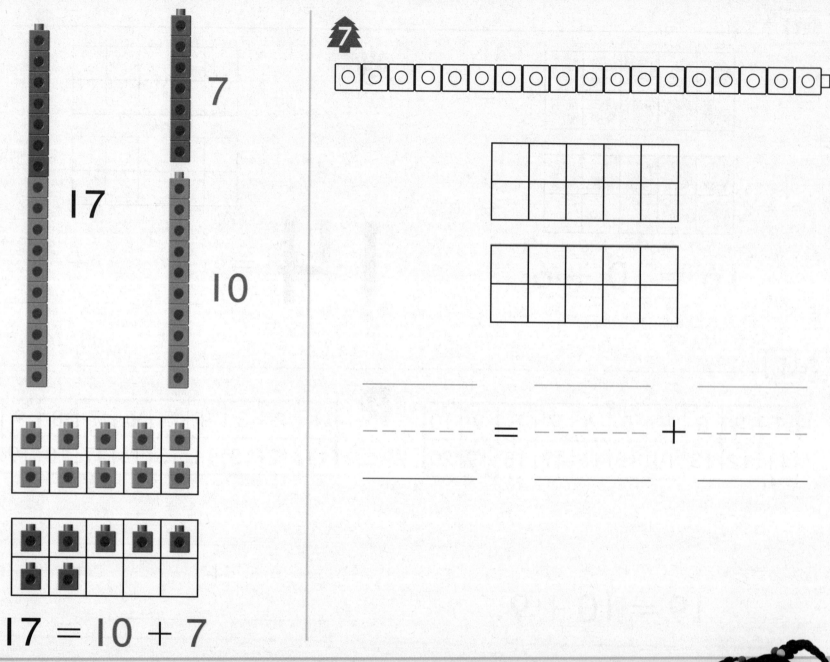

17

7

10

17 = 10 + 7

Directions Have students: ⤷ color 10 cubes blue in the train to show 10 ones, and then draw 10 blue cubes in the top ten-frame. Have them color the remaining cubes in the train red to show more ones, count them, and then draw the same number of red cubes in the bottom ten-frame. Then have them write an equation to match the pictures.

Name _____

1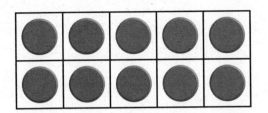

Ⓐ $16 = 10 + 6$

Ⓑ $15 = 10 + 5$

Ⓒ $14 = 10 + 4$

Ⓓ $13 = 10 + 3$

2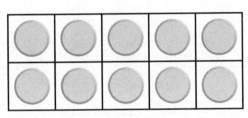

Ⓐ 10 and 6

Ⓑ 10 and 7

Ⓒ 10 and 8

Ⓓ 10 and 9

_____ + _____ = 18

3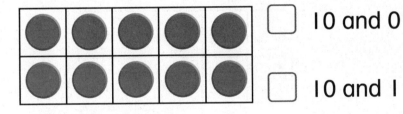

☐ 10 and 0

☐ 10 and 1

☐ 10 and 2

☐ 10 and 3

$12 =$ _____ $+$ _____

Directions Have students mark the best answer. **1** Which equation matches the counters in the double ten-frame? **2** Which numbers complete the equation and match the counters in the double ten-frame? **3** Mark all the ways that could complete the equation.

4

1	2	3	4	5	6	7	8	9	10
11	12	13	14	15	16	17	18	19	20

_____ + _____ = _____

5

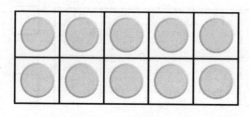

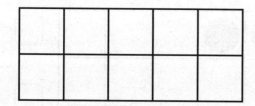

13 = _ _ _ _ + _ _ _ _

Directions Have students: **4** find the number with the blue box around it, and then color the number that is 10 greater than the number in the blue box. Then have them write an equation to match; **5** draw counters to make 13, and then complete the equation to match the picture.

Name _____

10 + 6 = 16

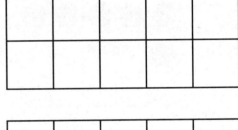

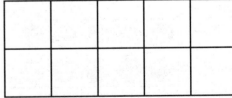

_____ = _____ + _____

Directions Have students: 6 draw counters to match the equation; 7 color 10 cubes blue to show 10 ones, and then draw 10 blue cubes in the top ten-frame. Have them color the remaining cubes in the train red to show more ones, count them, and then draw the same number of red cubes in the bottom ten-frame. Then have them write an equation to match the pictures.

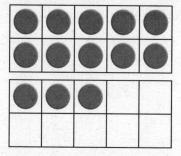

$$11 = 10 + 1$$

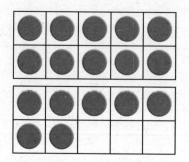

$$14 = 10 + 4$$

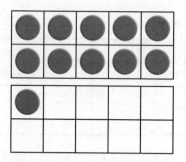

$$13 = 10 + 3$$

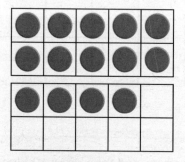

$$17 = 10 + 7$$

Directions 8 Have students draw a line from each double ten-frame to the equation that matches.

Name _____

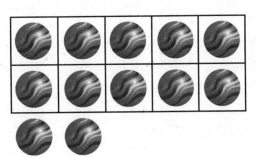

_ _ _ _ _ _ _   +   _ _ _ _ _ _ _   =   _ _ _ _ _ _ _
_ _ _ _ _ _ _   _ _ _ _ _ _ _   _ _ _ _ _ _ _

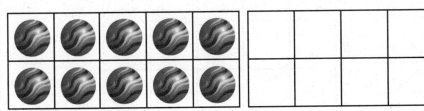

18 = _ _ _ _ _ _   +   _ _ _ _ _ _

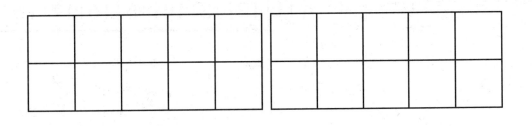

_ _ _ _ _ _   =   _ _ _ _ _ _   +   _ _ _ _ _ _   _ _ _ _ _ _   +   _ _ _ _ _ _   =   _ _ _ _ _ _

Directions Mason's Marbles Say: *Mason collects many different kinds of marbles. He uses ten-frames to help count his marbles.* Have students: ★ write the equation to show how many purple marbles Mason has; ❷ draw red marbles in the second ten-frame to show 18 red marbles in all, and then complete the equation. Have them tell how the picture and equation show 10 ones and some more ones; ❸ draw 17 yellow marbles in the double ten-frame, and then write two equations to match their drawing.

4

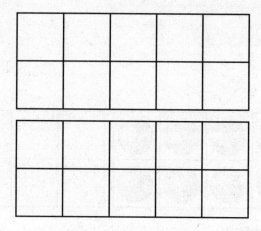

$$10 + 3 = 13$$

1	2	3	4	5	6	7	8	9	10
11	12	13	14	15	16	17	18	19	20

_____   _____

- - - - -   - - - - - **+** - - - - - **=** - - - - -

_____   _____   _____   _____

Directions ♥ Have students look at the equation Mason wrote to show how many green marbles he has, and then draw the marbles in the double ten-frame to show the number. Have them tell how the picture shows 10 ones and some more ones. ✋ Say: *Mason put his striped marbles in a five-frame. Then he buys 10 more striped marbles.* Have students write the number to tell how many striped marbles Mason had at first, and then color the part of the number chart to show how many striped marbles he has now. Then have them write an equation to tell how many striped marbles he has in all. Ask them to explain how the picture and equation show 10 ones and some more ones.

© Pearson Education, Inc. K

Topic 10 | Performance Assessment

Count Numbers to 100

Essential Question: How can numbers to 100 be counted using a hundred chart?

Digital Resources

Solve · Learn · Glossary

Tools · Assessment · Help · Games

Ants

Ants live in colonies.

Math and Science Project: Ant Colonies

Directions Read the character speech bubbles to students. **Find Out!** Have students find out how ants live and work together in colonies. Say: *Talk to friends and relatives about ant colonies. Ask about the different jobs ants in a colony might have that help them survive.* **Journal: Make a Poster** Have students make a poster. Have them draw an ant colony with 5 groups of ants. There should be 10 ants in each group. Then have them count by tens to find how many ants there are in all. Have students use a hundred chart to practice counting by tens to 50.

Name _____

Review What You Know

1

11   17   19

2

10 + 6

3 + 10

3

10 + 4

8 + 10

4

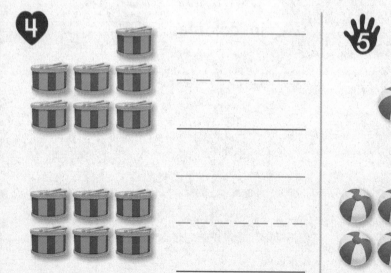

_____

- - - - - - - - - - -

_____

- - - - - - - - - - -

5

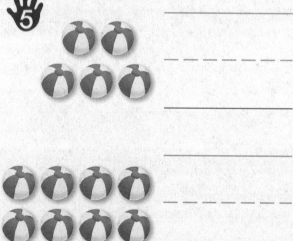

_____

- - - - - - - - - - -

_____

- - - - - - - - - - -

6

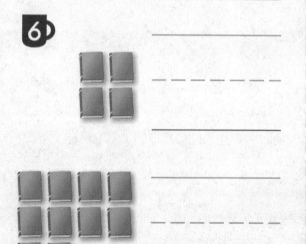

_____

- - - - - - - - - - -

_____

- - - - - - - - - - -

Directions Have students: ⭐ draw a circle around the number *nineteen*; 🍎 draw a circle around the addition expression that makes 16; 🐦 draw a circle around the addition expression that makes 18; ✋–☕ count each set of objects, write the numbers to tell how many, and then draw a circle around the number that is greater than the other number.

       Topic 11

My Word Cards

Directions Have students cut out the vocabulary cards. Read the front of the card, and then ask them to explain what the word or phrase means.

A-Z Glossary

pattern

ones

tens

column

hundred chart

decade

Directions Review the definitions and have students study the cards. Extend learning by having students draw pictures for each word on a separate piece of paper.

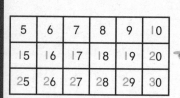

5	6	7	8	9	10
15	16	17	18	19	20
25	26	27	28	29	30

Point to the colored numbers.
Say: *The number to the left of the ones are the* **tens.** *We count up by 10 when we count by* **tens.** *9...19...29...*

5	6	7	8	9	10
15	16	17	18	19	20
25	26	27	28	29	30

Point to the colored numbers.
Say: *When we count 5...6...7...8...9 we are counting by* **ones.**

10 20 30 40 50

Point to the numbers.
Say: *When you count by tens you are using a number* **pattern.**

1	2	3	4	5	6	7	8	9	10
11	12	13	14	15	16	17	18	19	20
21	22	23	24	25	26	27	28	29	30
31	32	33	34	35	36	37	38	39	40
41	42	43	44	45	46	47	48	49	50
51	52	53	54	55	56	57	58	59	60
61	62	63	64	65	66	67	68	69	70
71	72	73	74	75	76	77	78	79	80
81	82	83	84	85	86	87	88	89	90
91	92	93	94	95	96	97	98	99	100

Point to the shaded column.
Say: *The* **decade** *numbers are the numbers counted when counting by tens to 100.*

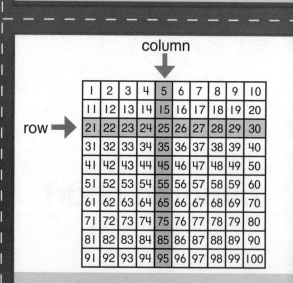

column

row

Point to the hundred chart.
Say: *A* **hundred chart** *helps us count larger numbers and find number patterns.*

1	2	3	4	5
11	12	13	14	15
21	22	23	24	25
31	32	33	34	35

Point to the circled column.
Say: *This is a* **column.** *Columns go up and down.*

© Pearson Education, Inc. K

Solve & Share

Name _____

1	2	3	4	5	6	7	8	9	10
11	12	13	14	15	16	17	18	19	20
21	22	23	24	25	26	27	28	29	30

Directions Say: *Count aloud to 30 while you point to each number. What patterns do you see or hear when you count to 30 using the numbers on the chart? Color the boxes that show a pattern you find.*

I can ...
use patterns to count to 30.

I can also look for patterns.

 Guided Practice

1

1	2	3	4	5	6	7	8	9	10
11	12	13	14	15	16	17	18	19	20
21	22	23	24	25	26	27	28	29	30

2

Directions Have students: **1** count aloud all the numbers in the top row. Have them listen to the following numbers in the bottom row, and then draw a circle around the number in the top row and the part of the number in the bottom row that sound alike: *twenty-ONE, twenty-TWO, twenty-THREE, twenty-FOUR, twenty-FIVE, twenty-SIX.* **2** listen to the following numbers, and then complete the numbers in the chart: *twenty-seven, twenty-eight, twenty-nine.*

3

					6	7	8	9	10
11	12	13	14	15	16	17	18	19	20
21	22	23	24	2_	2_	2_	2_	2_	30

4 (heart icon)

5 (hand icon)

1	2	3		5	6	7	8	9	10
11	12	13		15	16				
21	22	23	2_	25	26	27	28	29	30

6 (mug icon)

Directions **3 Number Sense** Have students write the missing numbers, and then explain how they know the numbers are correct. Have students: **4** count the numbers in the bottom row aloud, and then write the missing numbers as they say them; **5** write the missing numbers in the column, say them aloud, and then explain how the numbers in that column are alike; **6** use the chart to find the missing numbers in the middle row, and then explain how they used the chart.

1	2	3	4	5	6		8	9	10
11	12	13	14	15	16		18	19	20
21	2_	2_	2_	2_	26	2_	28	29	30

1	2	3	4	5	6	7	8	9	10
11	12							19	20
21	22	23	24	25	26	27	28	29	30

Directions Have students: ✿ write the missing numbers in the column, say them aloud, and then explain how the numbers in that column are alike; ⚑ count the numbers in the bottom row aloud, and then write the missing numbers as they say them aloud. ◆ **Higher Order Thinking** Have students write the missing numbers on the chart, count them aloud, and then explain the pattern they hear. Then have them draw a circle around the other number that fits the pattern.

Topic 11 | Lesson 1

Name _____

Another Look!

1	2	3	4	5	6	7	8	9	10
11	12	13	14	15	16	17	18	19	20
21	22	23	24	25	26	27	28	29	30

HOME ACTIVITY Tell your child a number between 1 and 10. Ask him or her to count up to 30 from that number.

1	2	3	4	5	6	7	8	9	10
11	12	13	14	15	16	17	18	19	20
21	22	23	24	25	26	27	28	29	30

Directions Say: *Listen to these numbers, and then draw a circle around the numbers in the chart that you hear:* nine, nineteen, twenty-nine. *What number do you see in each box of the column? What number do you hear in each number?* Have students listen to the numbers, and then draw a circle around the numbers in the chart that they hear: ⭐ *four, fourteen, twenty-four;* 🍎 *sixteen, seventeen, eighteen, nineteen.*

Topic 11 | Lesson 1

Digital Resources at PearsonRealize.com

six hundred twenty-nine **629**

	2	3	4	5	6	7	8	9	10
	12	13	14	15	16	17	18	19	20
2_	22	23	24	25	26	27	28	29	30

1	2	3	4	5	6	7	8	9	10
11	12	13	14	15	16	17	18	19	20
21	22	23	24	25	26	27	28	29	30

Directions Have students: ✦ write the missing numbers in the column, say them aloud, and then explain how the numbers in that column are alike; ♥ listen to the numbers, and then draw a circle around the numbers in the chart that they hear: *twenty-seven, twenty-eight, twenty-nine, thirty;* ✋ listen to the numbers, and then draw a circle around the numbers in the chart that they hear: *twenty, twenty-one, twenty-two, twenty-three.* ☕ **Higher Order Thinking** Have students count aloud the numbers in the middle row. Have them color the boxes of the numbers that do NOT fit the pattern, and then explain why they do NOT fit the pattern.

Solve & Share

Name _____

Solve

1	2	3	4	5	6	7	8	9	10
11	12	13	14	15	16	17	18	19	20
21	22						28	29	30
31	32	33	34	35	36	37	38	39	40
41	42	43	44	45	46	47	48	49	50

Directions Say: *Look at the numbers on the chart and the parts that are underlined. Count aloud all the numbers to 50. Write and then say the numbers that are missing. Tell how you know the numbers are correct.*

I can ... use patterns to count to 50.

I can also look for patterns.

1	2	3	4	5	6	7	8	9	●
11	12	13	14	15	16	17	18	19	●
21	22	23	24	25	26	27	28	29	●
31	32	33	34	35	36	37	38	39	●
41	42	43	44	45	46	47	48	49	●

1	2	3	4	5	6	7	8	9	10
11	12	13	14	15	16	17	18	19	20
21	22	23	24	25	26	27	28	29	30
31	32	33	○	○	○	○	○	39	40
41	42	43	44	45	46	47	48	49	50

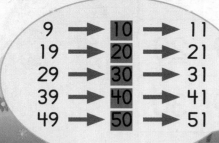

9 → **10** → 11
19 → **20** → 21
29 → **30** → 31
39 → **40** → 41
49 → **50** → 51

33 → 34 → 35 → 36 → 37 → 38 → 39

☆ Guided Practice

21	22	23	24	25	26	27	28	29	30
31	32	33	34	35	36	37	38	39	40
41	42	43	44	45	46	47	48	49	50

 (★ 1)

 (🍎 2)

Directions Have students: count aloud the numbers in the top row. Then have them count all the numbers in the middle row aloud, and draw a circle around the part of the number that sounds the same; ❷ complete the numbers in the bottom row as they count the numbers aloud, and then explain how they knew which number to write in the tens place.

Name _____

❸

	2	3	4		6	7	8	9	10
11	12	13	14	15		17	_8	19	20
21	22	23	24	25	26	27	_8	29	30
31	32	33	34				_8	39	40
41	42	43	44	45	46	47	_8	49	50

❹

✋5

❻ _____
- - - - - - -
_____

🌲7   34 35 36   26 36 46   35 36 37

Directions Have students: ❸ write the missing numbers in the first two rows, and then explain how they found the numbers; ❹ color the boxes of the numbers that have 2 in the tens place; ✋5 find and mark an X on these numbers: *thirty-two, forty-four.* ❻ **Vocabulary** Have students complete the numbers in the green column, explain the **pattern** they see in the tens place, and then write the number that is always the same in that column. ❼ Have students find the blue boxes on the chart, and then circle the set of numbers that shows the missing numbers.

Independent Practice

8

1	2			5		7	8	9	
11		13	14	15	16		18	19	
21	22	23	24	25	26	27	28	29	
31	32	33	34	35	36	37	38	39	40
41	42	43	44	45	46	47	48	49	

9 10

Directions Have students: **8** write all the missing numbers in the chart, and then explain how they found the numbers; **9** color the boxes of the numbers that have 4 in the tens place; **10** find and mark an X on the following numbers: *thirty-five, forty-one, forty-eight.* **Higher Order Thinking** Have students look at the green column, write all the numbers that are in the column, and then explain how they used the number chart to find the answer.

     Topic 11 | Lesson 2

Name _____

Another Look!

1	2	3	4	5	6	7	8	9	10
11	12	13	14	15	16	17	18	19	20
21	22	23	24	25	26	27	28	29	30
31	32	33	34	35	36	37	38	39	40
41	42	43	44	45	46	47	48	49	50

HOME ACTIVITY Tell your child a number under 50. Ask him or her to count from that number up to 50. Repeat with different numbers.

 ⭐ ❷

1	2	3	4	5	6	7	8	9	10
11	12	13	14	15	16	17	18	19	20
21	22	23	24	25	26	27	28	29	30
31	32	33	34	35	36	37	38	39	40
41	42	43	44	45	46	47	48	49	50

Directions Have students point to the fourth row. Say: *Listen to the following numbers, and then draw a circle around the numbers in the chart that you hear:* thirty-three, thirty-four, thirty-five, thirty-six, thirty-seven. *What number do you see in almost every box of this row? What number do you hear in those numbers?* Have students listen to the numbers, draw a circle around the numbers in the chart that they hear, and then tell what is repeated in each number: ⭐ *twenty-six, twenty-seven, twenty-eight, twenty-nine;* ❷ *forty-one, forty-two, forty-three, forty-four.*

3

1	2	3	4	5					10
11	12	13	14	15	16	17	18	19	20
21	22	23	24	25	26	27	28	29	30
31	32	33	34	35	36	37	38	39	40
41	42	43	44	45	46	47	48	49	50

4

5

Directions Have students: **3** write the missing numbers in the top row, say them aloud, and then explain how they know they are correct; **4** look at the numbers in the top row with a circle drawn around them. Then have them draw a circle around the tens place in each column that matches the pattern of those numbers. Have them count the numbers aloud, and then explain the pattern they hear. **Higher Order Thinking** Have students listen to the numbers, and then write the numbers they hear: *ten, twenty, thirty, forty, fifty.*

© Pearson Education, Inc. K **Topic 11** | Lesson 2

Solve & Share

Name _____

Solve

1	2	3	4	5	6	7	8	9	10
11	12	13	14	15	16	17	18	19	20
21	22	23	24	25	26	27	28	29	30
31	32	33	34	35	36	37	38	39	40
41	42	43	44	45	46	47	48	49	50
51	52	53	54	55	56	57	58	59	60
61	62	63	64	65	66	67	68	69	70
71	72	73	74	75	76	77	78	79	80
81	82	83	84	85	86	87	88	89	90
91	92	93	94	95	96	97	98	99	100

Directions Say: *Color all the boxes of the numbers that have a zero in the ones place as you count them aloud. Tell how you know which numbers to count.*

I can ...
skip count by tens to 100.

I can also look for patterns.

1	2	3	4	5	6	7	8	9	10
11	12	13	14	15	16	17	18	19	20
21	22	23	24	25	26	27	28	29	30
31	32	33	34	35	36	37	38	39	40
41	42	43	44	45	46	47	48	49	50
51	52	53	54	55	56	57	58	59	60

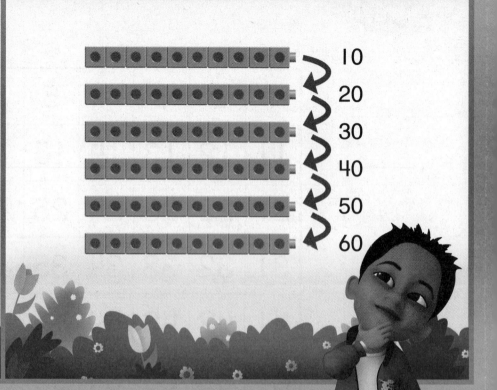

☆ Guided Practice

1

1	2	3	4	5	6	7	8	9	10
11	12	13	14	15	16	17	18	19	20
21	22	23	24	25	26	27	28	29	(30)
31	32	33	34	35	36	37	38	39	40
41	42	43	44	45	46	47	48	49	50
51	52	53	54	55	56	57	58	59	60

2

51	52	53	54	55	56	57	58	59	60
61	62	63	64	65	66	67	68	69	
71	72	73	74	75	76	77	78	79	80
81	82	83	84	85	86	87	88	89	90
91	92	93	94	95	96	97	98	99	100

50   60   (70)

Directions Have students: **1** draw a circle around the decade number that comes before 40 but after 20; **2** look at the chart, and then draw a circle around the missing number.

© Pearson Education, Inc. K

Name _____

3

1	2	3	4	5	6	7	8	9	10
11	12	13	14	15	16	17	18	19	20
21	22	23	24	25	26	27	28	29	30
31	32	33	34	35	36	37	38	39	40
41	42	43	44	45	46	47	48	49	50
51	52	53	54	55	56	57	58	59	60
61	62	63	64	65	66	67	68	69	70
71	72	73	74	75	76	77	78	79	80
81	82	83	84	85	86	87	88	89	90
91	92	93	94	95	96	97	98	99	100

4

20   30   50

5

40   60   70

6

80   90   100

Directions Have students: **3** draw a circle around the missing numbers in the following pattern: *ten, twenty, thirty,* ____, *fifty,* ____, *seventy,* ____, ____, *one hundred;* **4**–**6** count the cubes, and then draw a circle around the number that tells how many.

Independent Practice

7 ▲

_____

_____

_____

_____

_____

_____

60   80   100

8 ⚑

_____

_____

_____

_____

60   80   100

9 ✎

_____   _____

- - - - - - - - - - - - - - - -   - - - - - - - - - - - - - - - -

_____   _____

- - - - - - - - - - - - - - - -   - - - - - - - - - - - - - - - -

_____   _____

Directions ▲ **Algebra** Have students count the cube trains by tens, write the decade numbers as they count, and then circle the number that tells how many. **8** Have students count the cubes, and then draw a circle around the number that tells how many. ✎ **Higher Order Thinking** Have students write all the decade numbers in order.

Name _____

Another Look!

1	2	3	4	5	6	7	8	9	10
11	12	13	14	15	16	17	18	19	20
21	22	23	24	25	26	27	28	29	30
31	32	33	34	35	36	37	38	39	40
41	42	43	44	45	46	47	48	49	50
51	52	53	54	55	56	57	58	59	60
61	62	63	64	65	66	67	68	69	70
71	72	73	74	75	76	77	78	79	80
81	82	83	84	85	86	87	88	89	90
91	92	93	94	95	96	97	98	99	100

HOME ACTIVITY Arrange 30 objects, such as pennies, beads, or other small objects, in groups of 10 on a table. Ask your child to use decade numbers to count the number of objects aloud. Repeat with up to 10 groups of objects.

1	2	3	4	5	6	7	8	9	10
11	12	13	14	15	16	17	18	19	20
21	22	23	24	25	26	27	28	29	30
31	32	33	34	35	36	37	38	39	40
41	42	43	44	45	46	47	48	49	50
51	52	53	54	55	56	57	58	59	60
61	62	63	64	65	66	67	68	69	70
71	72	73	74	75	76	77	78	79	80
81	82	83	84	85	86	87	88	89	90
91	92	93	94	95	96	97	98	99	100

Directions Say: *Color green the boxes of the following decade numbers:* ten, forty, fifty, sixty, ninety. ⭐ Have students color orange the boxes of the following decade numbers: *twenty, thirty, fifty, seventy, eighty, one hundred.*

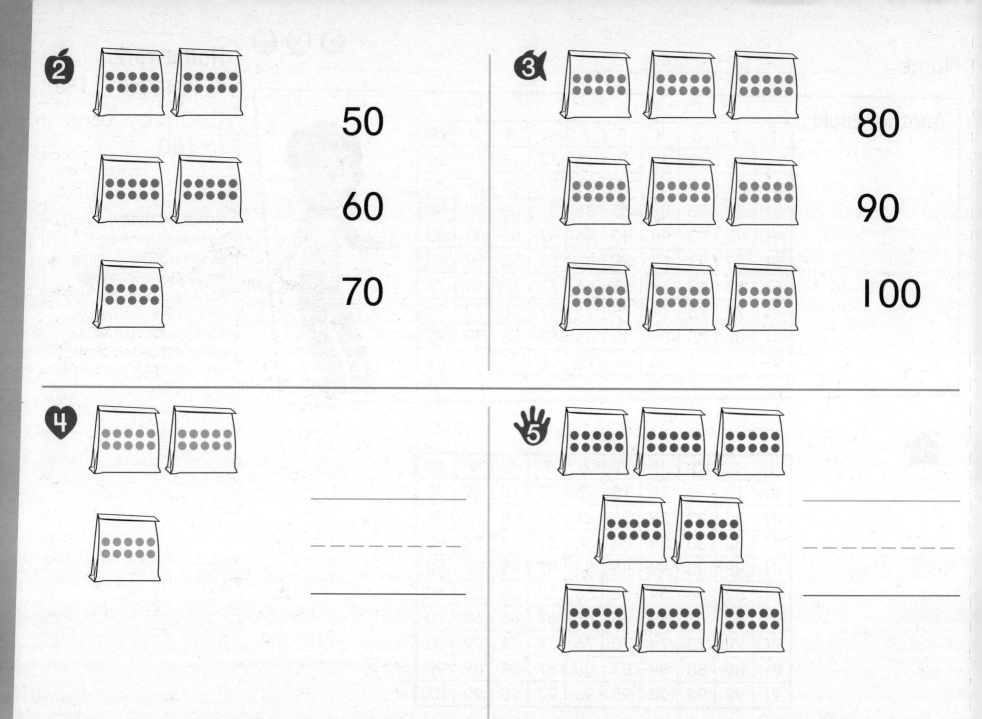

2

50

60

70

3

80

90

100

4

5

Directions **2** and **3** Have students count the dots, and then draw a circle around the number that tells how many. **4** **Higher Order Thinking** Have students count the number of dots, and then write the number to tell how many. **5** **Higher Order Thinking** Have students count the number of dots, and then write the number to tell how many.

642 six hundred forty-two © Pearson Education, Inc. K **Topic 11** | Lesson 3

Name _____

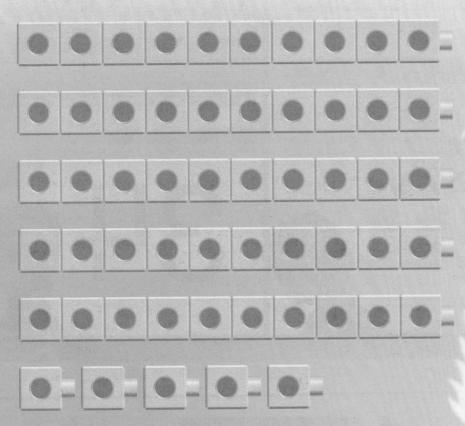

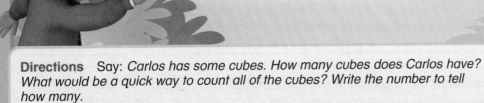

Directions Say: *Carlos has some cubes. How many cubes does Carlos have? What would be a quick way to count all of the cubes? Write the number to tell how many.*

I can ...
count to the number 100 by using tens and ones.

I can also reason about math.

10
20
30

31 32 33 34

34

☆ Guided Practice

1

77

(87)

97

2

46

47

48

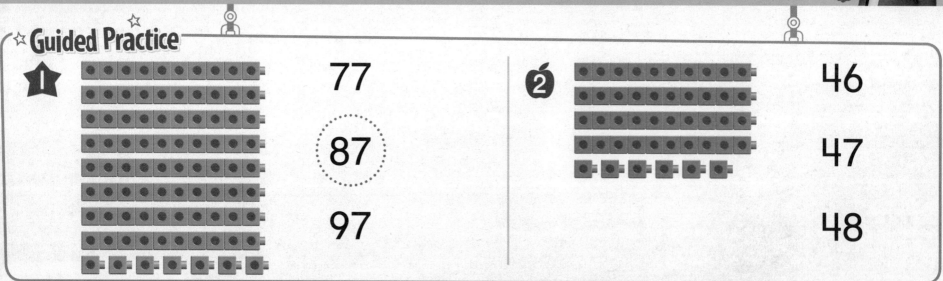

Directions ⭐ and ❷ Have students count by tens and by ones, and then draw a circle around the number that tells how many. Remind students that they can use a hundred chart to count by tens and by ones.

© Pearson Education, Inc. K

Name _____

3

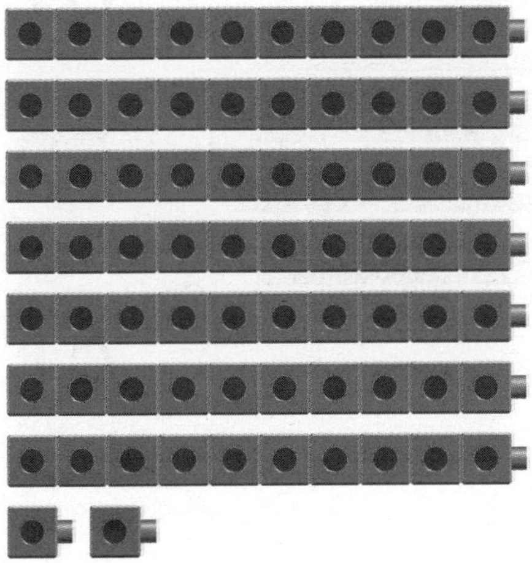

52

62

72

4

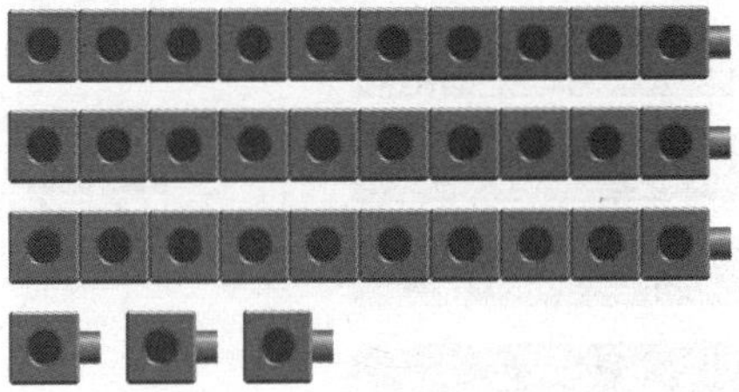

23

32

33

5

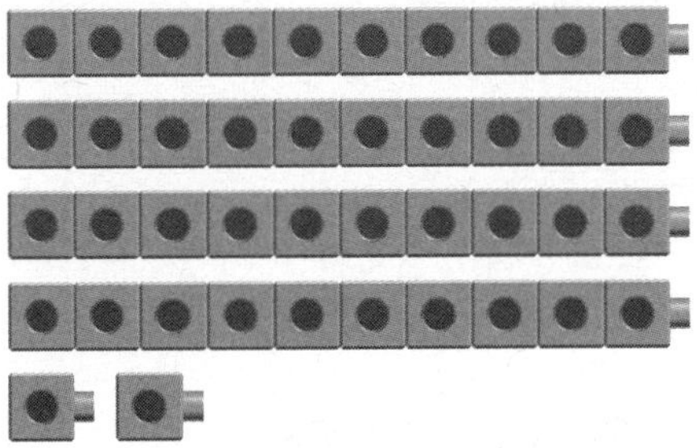

42

43

52

6

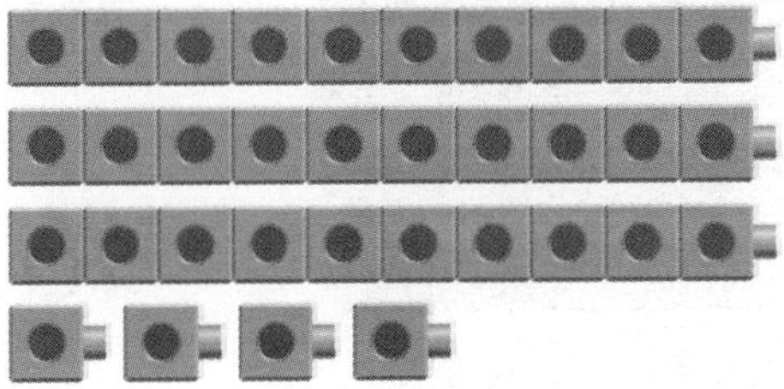

33

34

35

Directions **3**—**6** Have students count by tens and by ones, and then draw a circle around the number that tells how many. If needed, allow students to use a hundred chart.

Independent Practice

 7

68

77

86

 **8**

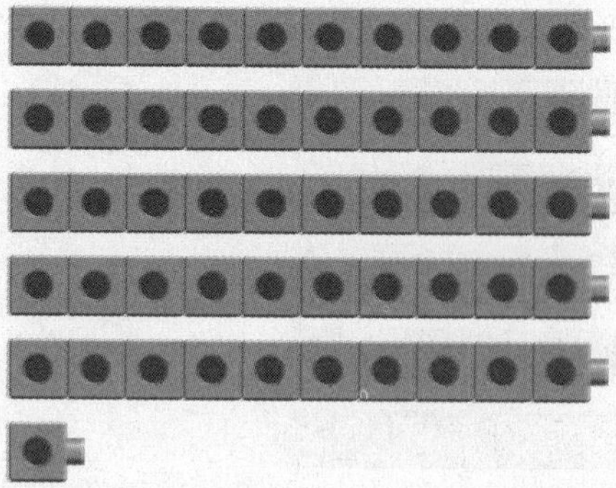

51

52

61

9

36

46

56

10

25

Directions **7**–**9** Have students count by tens and by ones, and then draw a circle around the number that tells how many.
10 **Higher Order Thinking** Have students draw cubes to show how to arrange the number 25 for easy counting.

© Pearson Education, Inc. K **Topic 11** | **Lesson 4**

Name _____

Another Look!

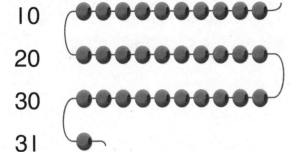

10

20

30

31

21   (31)   41

HOME ACTIVITY Set out a large number of pennies, beads, or other small objects. Have your child arrange the objects in groups of 10 for fast counting. Then have him or her count by tens and by ones to find how many.

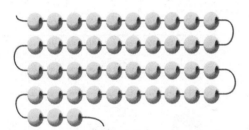

34   42   43

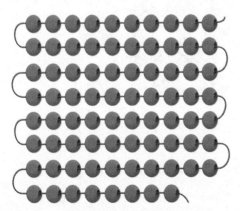

78   87   88

Directions Say: *Alex arranged his counting beads into groups of 10 for easy counting. Count the beads by tens and then by ones. How many beads are there? Draw a circle around the number that tells how many.* ⭐ and ❷ Have students count the beads by tens and by ones, and then draw a circle around the number that tells how many.

③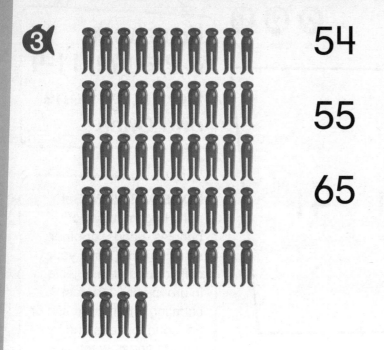

54

55

65

④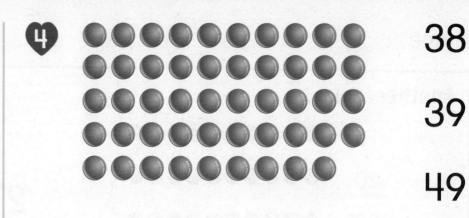

38

39

49

⑤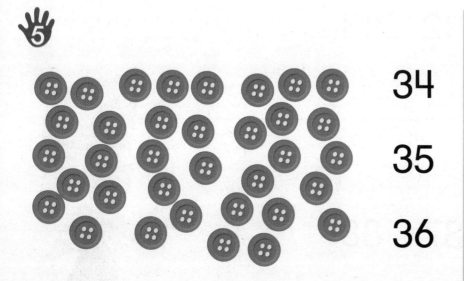

34

35

36

⑥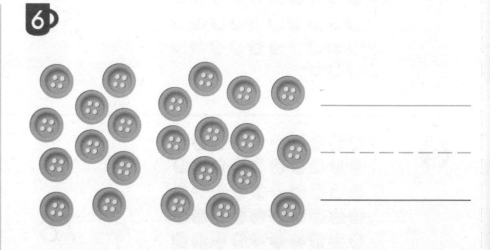

_____

_ _ _ _ _ _ _

_____

Name _____

Solve

1	2	3	4	5	6	7	8	9	10
11	12	13	14	15	16	17	18	19	20
21	22	23	24	25	26	27	28	29	30
31	32	33	34	35	36	37	38	39	40
41	42	43	44	45	46	47	48	49	50
51	52	53	54	55	56	57	58	59	60
61	62	63	64	65	66	67	68	69	70
71	72	73	74	75	76	77	78	79	80
81	82	83	84	85	86	87	88	89	90
91	92	93	94	95	96	97	98	99	100

Directions Say: *Count forward from the yellow number. Stop at the red number. Tell how many numbers you counted aloud. Color the boxes of the numbers you counted aloud to show your work.*

I can ...
count forward from any number to 100 by ones.

I can also make sense of problems.

72

71	72	73	74	75	76	77	78	79	80
81	82	83	84	85	86	87	88	89	90
91	92	93	94	95	96	97	98	99	100

91

☆ Guided Practice

21	22	23	24	25	26	27	28	29	30
31	32	33	34	35	36	37	38	39	40
41	42	43	44	45	46	47	48	49	50
51	52	53	54	55	56	57	58	59	60

1	2	3	4	5	6	7	8	9	10
11	12	13	14	15	16	17	18	19	20
21	22	23	24	25	26	27	28	29	30
31	32	33	34	35	36	37	38	39	40

Directions ★ and ❷ Have students color the boxes of the numbers as they count aloud, starting at the yellow box and ending at the red box.

3

1	2	3	4	5	6	7	8	9	10
11	12	13	14	15	16	17	18	19	20
21	22	23	24	25	26	27	28	29	30
31	32	33	34	35	36	37	38	39	40
41	42	43	44	45	46	47	48	49	50
51	52	53	54	55	56	57	58	59	60
61	62	63	64	65	66	67	68	69	70
71	72	73	74	75	76	77	78	79	80
81	82	83	84	85	86	87	88	89	90
91	92	93	94	95	96	97	98	99	100

 4

1	2	3	4	5	6	7	8	9	10
11	12	13	14	15	16	17	18	19	20
21	22	23	24	25	26	27	28	29	30
31	32	33	34	35	36	37	38	39	40
41	42	43	44	45	46	47	48	49	50
51	52	53	54	55	56	57	58	59	60
61	62	63	64	65	66	67	68	69	70
71	72	73	74	75	76	77	78	79	80
81	82	83	84	85	86	87	88	89	90
91	92	93	94	95	96	97	98	99	100

 5

1	2	3	4	5	6	7	8	9	10
11	12	13	14	15	16	17	18	19	20
21	22	23	24	25	26	27	28	29	30
31	32	33	34	35	36	37	38	39	40
41	42	43	44	45	46	47	48	49	50
51	52	53	54	55	56	57	58	59	60
61	62	63	64	65	66	67	68	69	70
71	72	73	74	75	76	77	78	79	80
81	82	83	84	85	86	87	88	89	90
91	92	93	94	95	96	97	98	99	100

 6

1	2	3	4	5	6	7	8	9	10
11	12	13	14	15	16	17	18	19	20
21	22	23	24	25	26	27	28	29	30
31	32	33	34	35	36	37	38	39	40
41	42	43	44	45	46	47	48	49	50
51	52	53	54	55	56	57	58	59	60
61	62	63	64	65	66	67	68	69	70
71	72	73	74	75	76	77	78	79	80
81	82	83	84	85	86	87	88	89	90
91	92	93	94	95	96	97	98	99	100

Directions **3**–**6** Have students color the boxes of the numbers as they count aloud, starting at the yellow box and ending at the red box.

Independent Practice

1	2	3	4	5	6	7	8	9	10
11	12	13	14	15	16	17	18	19	20
21	22	23	24	25	26	27	28	29	30
31	32	33	34	35	36	37	38	39	40
41	42	43	44	45	46	47	48	49	50
51	52	53	54	55	56	57	58	59	60
61	62	63	64	65	66	67	68	69	70
71	72	73	74	75	76	77	78	79	80
81	82	83	84	85	86	87	88	89	90
91	92	93	94	95	96	97	98	99	100

 8

1	2	3	4	5	6	7	8	9	10
11	12	13	14	15	16	17	18	19	20
21	22	23	24	25	26	27	28	29	30
31	32	33	34	35	36	37	38	39	40
41	42	43	44	45	46	47	48	49	50
51	52	53	54	55	56	57	58	59	60
61	62	63	64	65	66	67	68	69	70
71	72	73	74	75	76	77	78	79	80
81	82	83	84	85	86	87	88	89	90
91	92	93	94	95	96	97	98	99	100

1	2	3	4	5	6	7	8	9	10
11	12	13	14	15	16	17	18	19	20
21	22	23	24	25	26	27	28	29	30
31	32	33	34	35	36	37	38	39	40
41	42	43	44	45	46	47	48	49	50
51	52	53	54	55	56	57	58	59	60
61	62	63	64	65	66	67	68	69	70
71	72	73	74	75	76	77	78	79	80
81	82	83	84	85	86	87	88	89	90
91	92	93	94	95	96	97	98	99	100

10

51	52	53	54	55	56	57	58	59	
61	62	63	64	65	66	67	68	69	
71	72	73	74	75	76	77	78	79	
81	82	83	84	85	86	87	88	89	
91	92	93	94	95	96	97	98	99	

Directions 7–9 Have students color the boxes of the numbers as they count aloud, starting at the yellow box and ending at the red box. 10 **Higher Order Thinking** Have students write the numbers as they count by tens aloud, starting at the yellow box and ending at the red box.

     Topic 11 | Lesson 5

Name _____

Another Look!

1	2	3	4	5	6	7	8	9	10
11	12	13	14	15	16	17	18	19	20
21	22	23	24	25	26	27	28	29	30
31	32	33	34	35	36	37	38	39	40
41	42	43	44	45	46	47	48	49	50
51	52	53	54	55	56	57	58	59	60
61	62	63	64	65	66	67	68	69	70
71	72	73	74	75	76	77	78	79	80
81	82	83	84	85	86	87	88	89	90
91	92	93	94	95	96	97	98	99	100

HOME ACTIVITY Point to a number on a hundred chart, such as 27. Have your child count from that number to another number you have chosen. Repeat with other numbers.

 1

1	2	3	4	5	6	7	8	9	10
11	12	13	14	15	16	17	18	19	20
21	22	23	24	25	26	27	28	29	30
31	32	33	34	35	36	37	38	39	40
41	42	43	44	45	46	47	48	49	50
51	52	53	54	55	56	57	58	59	60
61	62	63	64	65	66	67	68	69	70
71	72	73	74	75	76	77	78	79	80
81	82	83	84	85	86	87	88	89	90
91	92	93	94	95	96	97	98	99	100

 2

1	2	3	4	5	6	7	8	9	10
11	12	13	14	15	16	17	18	19	20
21	22	23	24	25	26	27	28	29	30
31	32	33	34	35	36	37	38	39	40
41	42	43	44	45	46	47	48	49	50
51	52	53	54	55	56	57	58	59	60
61	62	63	64	65	66	67	68	69	70
71	72	73	74	75	76	77	78	79	80
81	82	83	84	85	86	87	88	89	90
91	92	93	94	95	96	97	98	99	100

Directions Say: *You can count forward from any number. Find and draw a circle around the number* eighteen. *Count aloud until you reach the red box. Color the boxes of the numbers you counted aloud.* Have students draw a circle around the given number, and then color the boxes of the numbers as they count aloud, starting at the circled number and ending at the red box. Have them: **1** draw a circle around the number *eighty;* **2** draw a circle around the number *thirty-six.*

1	2	3	4	5	6	7	8	9	10
11	12	13	14	15	16	17	18	19	20
21	22	23	24	25	26	27	28	29	30
31	32	33	34	35	36	37	38	39	40
41	42	43	**44**	45	46	47	48	49	50
51	52	53	54	55	56	57	58	59	60
61	62	63	64	65	66	67	68	69	70
71	72	73	74	75	76	77	78	79	80
81	82	83	84	85	86	87	88	89	90
91	92	93	94	95	96	97	98	99	100

4

1	2	3	4	5	6	7	8	9	10
11	12	13	14	15	16	17	18	19	20
21	22	23	24	25	26	27	28	29	30
31	32	33	34	35	36	37	38	39	40
41	42	43	44	45	46	47	48	49	50
51	52	53	54	55	56	57	58	59	60
61	62	63	64	65	66	67	68	69	**70**
71	72	73	74	75	76	77	78	79	80
81	82	83	84	85	86	87	88	89	90
91	92	93	94	95	96	97	98	99	100

5

1	2	3	4	5	6	7	8	9	10
11	12	13	14	15	16	17	18	19	20
21	22	23	24	25	26	27	28	29	30
31	32	33	34	35	36	37	38	39	40
41	42	43	44	45	46	47	48	49	50
51	52	53	54	55	56	57	58	59	60
61	62	63	64	65	66	67	68	69	70
71	72	73	74	75	76	77	78	79	80
81	82	83	84	85	86	87	88	89	90
91	92	93	94	95	96	97	98	99	100

6

1	2	3	4	5	6	7	8	9	
11	12	13	14	15	16	17	18	19	
21	22	23	24	25	26	27	28	29	
31	32	33	34	35	36	37	38	39	
41	42	43	44	45	46	47	48	49	
51	52	53	54	55	56	57	58	59	
61	62	63	64	65	66	67	68	69	
71	72	73	74	75	76	77	78	79	
81	82	83	84	85	86	87	88	89	
91	92	93	94	95	96	97	98	99	

Directions Have students draw a circle around the given number, and then color the boxes of the numbers as they count aloud, starting at the circled number and ending at the red box. Have them: **3** draw a circle around the number *twenty-two*; **4** draw a circle around the number *fifty-one*. **5 Higher Order Thinking** Have students draw a circle around the number that comes after *sixteen*, the number that comes after *forty-eight*, and the number that comes after *eighty*. **6 Higher Order Thinking** Have students write the numbers as they count aloud by tens, starting at the yellow box and ending at the red box.

Solve & Share

Name _____

Solve

Lesson 11-6
Count Using
Patterns to 100

1	2	3	4	5	6	7	8	9	10
11	12	13	14	15	16	17	18	19	20
21	22	23	24	25	26	27	28	29	30
31	32	33	34	35	36	37	38	39	40
41	42	43	44	45	46	47	48	49	50
51	52	53	54	55	56	57	58	59	60
61	62	63	64	65	66	67	68	69	70
71	72	73	74	75	76	77	78	79	80
81	82	83	84	85	86	87	88	89	90
91	92	93	94	95	96	97	98	99	100

Directions Say: *Carlos looks at the chart. He knows 21 comes just after 20. Draw a circle around the numbers that come just after each decade number. How do you know you are correct? What patterns do you see?*

I can ...
count by tens and ones from any number up to 100.

I can also reason about math.

41	42	43	44	45	46	47	48	49	50
51	52	53	54	55	56	57	58	59	60
61	62	63	64	65	66	67	68	69	70
71	72	73	74	75	76	77	78	79	80
81	82	83	84	85	86	87	88	89	90
91	92	93	94	95	96	97	98	99	100

61	62	63	64	65	66	67	68	69	70
71	72	73	74	75	76	77	78	79	80
81	82	83	84	85	86	87	88	89	90
91	92	93	94	95	96	97	98	99	100

☆ Guided Practice

1

1	2	3	4	5	6	7	8	9	10
11	12	13	14	15	16	17	18	19	20
21	22	23	24	25	26	27	28	29	30

2

1	2	3	4	5	6	7	8	9	10
11	12	13	14	15	16	17	18	19	20
21	22	23	24	25	26	27	28	29	30

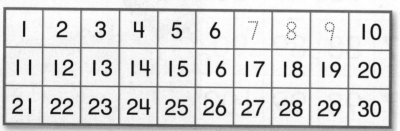

Directions 1 and 2 Have students count forward to find and write the missing numbers.

© Pearson Education, Inc. K

Topic 11 | Lesson 6

Name _____

61	62	63	64	65				69	70
71	72	73	74	75	76	77	78	79	80
81	82	83	84	85	86	87	88	89	90

66	76	86
67	68	69
66	67	68

42	43	44	45	46	47	48	49	50
52	53	54	55	56	57	58	59	60
62	63	64	65	66	67	68	69	70

41	42	43
41	51	61
41	43	45

31	32	33	34	35	36	37	38	39	
41	42	43	44	45	46	47	48	49	
51	52	53	54	55	56	57	58	59	

40	50	60
40	41	42
38	39	40

11	12	13	14	15	16	17	18	19	20
21	22	23	24	25	26	27	28	29	
	33	34	35	36	37	38	39	40

20	30	40
28	29	30
30	31	32

Directions ❸–❻ Have students count forward, and then draw a circle around the row that shows the missing set of numbers.

Independent Practice

 7

71	72	73	74	75	76	77	78	79	80
81	82	83	84	85	86	87	88	89	90
91	92	93	94	95	96	97			

80   90   100

98   99   100

89   99   100

8

51	52	53	54	55	56	57	58	59	60
61	62	63	64	65	66	67	68	69	70
71	72	73				77	78	79	80

74   84   94

74   64   54

74   75   76

 9

1	2	3	4	5		7	8	9	10
11	12	13	14	15		17	18	19	20
21	22	23	24	25		27	28	29	30

6   7   8

6   16   26

6   17   28

10

31	32	33	34	35	36	37	38	39	40
41	42	43	44	45	46	47	48	49	50
51						57	58	59	60
61	62	63	64	65	66	67	68	69	70
71	72	73	74	75	76	77	78	79	80

Directions **7**–**9** Have students count forward, and then draw a circle around the row that shows the missing set of numbers. **10 Higher Order Thinking** Have students count forward to find the missing numbers, write the missing numbers in the chart, and then draw a circle around the column that has 3 in the ones place.

         Topic 11 | Lesson 6

Name _____

Another Look!

1	2	3	4	5	6	7	8	9	10
11	12	13	14	15	16	17	18	19	20
21	22	23	24	25	26	27	28	29	30
31	32	33	34	35	36	37	38	39	40
41	42	43	44	45	46	47	48	49	50

HOME ACTIVITY Point to a hundred chart from this lesson. Take turns making up riddles and guessing the answers. For example, ask your child: *What number comes just after 31 and just before 33?* (32)

 1

1	2	3	4	5	6	7	8	9	10
11	12	13	14	15	16	17	18	19	20
21	22	23	24	25	26	27	28	29	30
31	32	33	34	35	36	37	38	39	40
41	42	43	44	45	46	47	48	49	50

2

1	2	3	4	5	6	7	8	9	10
11	12	13	14	15	16	17	18	19	20
21	22	23	24	25	26	27	28	29	30
31	32	33	34	35	36	37	38	39	40
41	42	43	44	45	46	47	48	49	50
51	52	53	54	55	56	57	58	59	60

Directions Say: *Draw a circle around the column with the numbers:* seven, seventeen, twenty-seven, thirty-seven, forty-seven. *What pattern do you see and hear?* Have students: **1** draw a circle around the column that has 9 in the ones place, count the numbers aloud, and then explain the pattern they see and hear; **2** draw a circle around the numbers that have 3 in the tens place, count the numbers aloud, and then explain the pattern they see and hear.

1	2	3	4	5	6	7	8	9	10
11	12	13	14	15	16	17	18	19	20
21	22	23	24	25	26	27	28	29	30
31	32	33	34	35	36	37	38	39	40
41	42	43	44	45	46	47	48	49	50

41	42	43	44	45	46	47	48	49	50
51	52	52	54	55	56	57	58	59	60
61	62	63	64	65	66	67	68	69	70
71	72	73	74	75	76	77	78	79	80
81	82	83	84	85	86	87	88	89	90
91	92	93	94	95	96	97	98	99	100

11		13		15	16	17	18	19	20
	22	23	24	25	26	27	28		30
	32		34	35	36	37	38		40
41	42	43		45	46	47	48		
51		53	54	55	56	57		59	60

51	52	53	54	55	56	57	58	59	60
61	62	63	64	65	66	67	68	69	70
71	72	73	74	75	76	77	78	79	80
81	82	83	84	85	86	87	88	89	90
91	92	93	94	95	96	97	98	99	100

Directions Have students: ❸ draw a circle around the row that starts with the number *twenty-one*, count the numbers aloud, and then explain the pattern they see and hear; ❹ draw a circle around the column that has 9 in the ones place, count the numbers aloud, and then explain the pattern they see and hear. ❺ **Higher Order Thinking** Have students count by ones to write the missing numbers, and then draw a circle around the column that has 4 in the ones place. ❻ **Higher Order Thinking** Have students draw a circle around the number that is 1 more than 72, and then mark an X on the number that is 1 less than 90.

© Pearson Education, Inc. K

Topic 11 | Lesson 6

1	2	3	4	5	6	7	8	9	10
11	12	13	14	15	16	17	18	19	20
21	22	23	24	25	26	27	28	29	30

1	2	3	4	5	6	7	8	9	10
11	12	13	14	15	16	17	18	19	20
21	22	23	24	25	26	27	28	29	30

Think.

Directions Say: *Carlos's teacher gives the class a challenge. Is there more than one way to solve it? Begin at 3. Use arrows and show how you could count up 15 places. Color the number red to show where you end. Show another way to use arrows on the second chart.*

I can ...
look for patterns to solve problems.

I can also count on by tens and by ones.

Top left number chart:

1	2	3	4	5	6	7	8	9	10
11	12	13	14	15	16	17	18	19	20
21	22	23	24	25	26	27	28	29	30
31	32	(33)	34	35	36	37	38	39	40

16 →

Top right number chart:

1	2	3	4	5	6	7	8	9	10
11	12	13	14	15	16	17	18	19	20
21	22	23	24	25	26	27	28	29	30
31	32	(33)	34	35	36	37	38	39	40

16 →

Both ways end at 33.

☆ Guided Practice

1

1	2	3	4	5	6	7	8	9	10
11	12	13	14	15	16	17	18	19	20
21	22	23	24	25	26	27	28	29	30
31	32	33	34	35	36	(37)	38	39	40

2

1	2	3	4	5	6	7	8	9	10
11	12	13	14	15	16	17	18	19	20
21	22	23	24	25	(26)	27	28	29	30
31	32	33	34	35	36	37	38	39	40

Directions Have students: **1** start at 22 and make a path to show how to count up 15 using only ones. Have them circle the number where they end, and then explain how they used the number chart to find the answer; **2** start at 12 and make a path to show how to count up 14 using tens and then ones. Have them circle the number where they end, and then explain how they used the number chart to find the answer.

© Pearson Education, Inc. K

Topic 11 | Lesson 7

Independent Practice

 3

41	42	43	44	45	46	47	48	49	50
51	52	53	54	55	56	57	58	59	60
61	62	63	64	65	66	67	68	69	70
71	72	73	74	75	76	77	78	79	80

 4

41	42	43	44	45	46	47	48	49	50
51	52	53	54	55	56	57	58	59	60
61	62	63	64	65	66	67	68	69	70
71	72	73	74	75	76	77	78	79	80

 5

61	62	63	64	65	66	67	68	69	70
71	72	73	74	75	76	77	78	79	80
81	82	83	84	85	86	87	88	89	90
91	92	93	94	95	96	97	98	99	100

 6

61	62	63	64	65	66	67	68	69	70
71	72	73	74	75	76	77	78	79	80
81	82	83	84	85	86	87	88	89	90
91	92	93	94	95	96	97	98	99	100

Directions Have students: **3** start at 42 and make a path to show how to count up 21 using ones and then tens. Have them circle the number where they end, and then explain how they used the number chart to find the answer; **4** start at 56 and make a path to show how to count up 15 using tens and ones. Have them circle the number where they end, and then explain how they used the number chart to find the answer; **5** start at 72 and make a path to show how to count up 27 in any way they choose. Have them circle the number where they end, and then explain how they used the number chart to find the answer; **6** start at 63 and make a path to show how to count up 22 in any way they choose. Have them draw a circle around the number where they end, and then explain how they know they are correct.

1	2	3	4	5	6	7	8	9	10
11	12	13	14	15	16	17	18	19	20
21	22	23	24	25	26	27	28	29	30
31	32	33	34	35	36	37	38	39	40

Directions Read the problem aloud. Then have students use multiple problem-solving methods to solve the problem. Say: *Start at 7 and count up 18 in any way you choose. Make a path to show how you counted, and then draw a circle around the number where you ended.* 🌲 **Be Precise** *How many tens are in 18?* 🎄 **Use Structure** *What numbers would you say if you only counted by ones? What numbers would you say if you counted by tens first and then by ones?* 🎄 **Generalize** *What number would you end on if you counted by ones first and then by tens? How do you know you are correct if you did NOT count again?*

Name _____

Another Look!

61	62	63	64	65	66	67	68	69	70
71	72	73	74	75	76	77	78	79	80
81	82	83	84	85	86	87	88	89	90
91	92	93	94	95	96	97	98	99	100

61	62	63	64	65	66	67	68	69	70
71	72	73	74	75	76	77	78	79	80
81	82	83	84	85	86	87	88	89	90
91	92	93	94	95	96	97	98	99	100

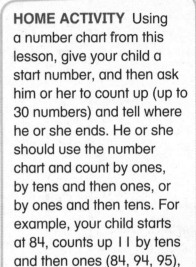

HOME ACTIVITY Using a number chart from this lesson, give your child a start number, and then ask him or her to count up (up to 30 numbers) and tell where he or she ends. He or she should use the number chart and count by ones, by tens and then ones, or by ones and then tens. For example, your child starts at 84, counts up 11 by tens and then ones (84, 94, 95), and ends on 95.

1

1	2	3	4	5	6	7	8	9	10
11	12	13	14	15	16	17	18	19	20
21	22	23	24	25	26	27	28	29	30
31	32	33	34	35	36	37	38	39	40

2

41	42	43	44	45	46	47	48	49	50
51	52	53	54	55	56	57	58	59	60
61	62	63	64	65	66	67	68	69	70
71	72	73	74	75	76	77	78	79	80

Directions Say: *Make a path to count up 25 from 72 by tens and ones. First count up by tens and then ones. Then count up by ones and then tens. Draw a circle around the number where you end.* Have students: **1** start at 19 and make a path to show how to count up 13 using only ones. Have them draw a circle around the number where they end, and then explain how they used the number chart to find the answer; **2** start at 41 and make a path to show how to count up 19 using tens and ones. Have them draw a circle around the number where they end, and then explain how they used the number chart to find the answer.

61	62	63	64	65	66	67	68	69	70
71	72	73	74	75	76	77	78	79	80
81	82	83	84	85	86	87	88	89	90
91	92	93	94	95	96	97	98	99	100

Directions Read the problem aloud. Then have students use multiple problem-solving methods to solve the problem. Say: *Start at 62 and count up 25 in any way you choose. Make a path to show how you counted, and then draw a circle around the number where you ended.* ❸ **Be Precise** *How many tens are in 25?* ❹ **Use Structure** *How would you use the number chart to help you count first by tens and then by ones?* ❺ **Generalize** *What number would you end on if you counted by ones first and then by tens? How do you know you are correct if you did NOT count again?*

1

G	B	I
$4+1$	$2+2$	$3-1$

$3+1$	$4-2$	$2+3$

2

T	A	C
$0+3$	$4-3$	$5-5$

$3-3$	$5-4$	$1+2$

Directions **1** and **2** Have students find a partner. Have them point to a clue in the top row, and then solve the addition or subtraction problem in the clue. Then have them look at the clues in the bottom row to find a match, and then write the clue letter above the match. Have students find a match for every clue.

I can ...
add and subtract fluently within 5.

1	2	3	4	5	6	7	8	9	10
11	12	13	14	15	16	17	18	19	20
21	22	23	24	25	26	27	28	29	30
31	32	33	34	35	36	37	38	39	40
41	42	43	44	45	46	47	48	49	50
51	52	53	54	55	56	57	58	59	60
61	62	63	64	65	66	67	68	69	70
71	72	73	74	75	76	77	78	79	80
81	82	83	84	85	86	87	88	89	90
91	92	93	94	95	96	97	98	99	100

Directions **Understand Vocabulary** Have students: ★ draw a circle around the part of the number in the orange column that is the **ones** place; ❷ draw a circle around the part of the number in the blue column that is the **tens** place; ❸ color the **decade** numbers yellow.

© Pearson Education, Inc. K

Name _____

①	②	③	④	⑤	⑥	⑦	⑧	⑨	⑩
⑪	⑫	⑬	⑭	⑮	⑯	⑰	⑱	⑲	20
21	22	23	24	25	26	27	28	29	30

1	2	3	4	5	6	7	8	9	10
11	12	13	14	15	16	17	18	19	20
21	22	23	24	25	26	27	28	29	30

Set B

41	42	43	44	45	46	47	48	49	50
51	52	53	54	55	56	57	58	59	60
61	62	63	64	65	66	67	68	69	70
71	72	73	74	75	76	77	78	79	80
81	82	83	84	85	86	87	88	89	90
91	92	93	94	95	96	97	98	99	100

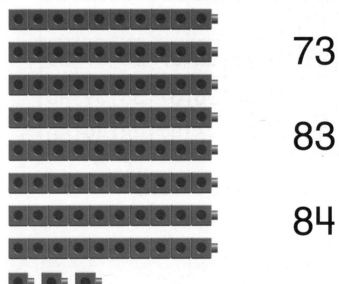

73

83

84

Directions Have students: ★ count aloud the numbers in the top row. Then have them count aloud the numbers in the bottom row and draw a circle around the number in the top row and the part of the number in the bottom row that sound the same; ② count by tens and ones, and then draw a circle around the number that tells how many.

1	2	3	4	5	6	7	8	9	10
11	12	13	14	15	16	17	18	19	20
21	22	23	24	25	26	27	28	29	30
31	32	33	34	35	36	37	38	39	40
41	42	43	44	45	46	47	48	49	50

3

51	52	53	54	55	56	57	58	59	60
61	62	63	64	65	66	67	68	69	70
71	72	73	74	75	76	77	78	79	80
81	82	83	84	85	86	87	88	89	90
91	92	93	94	95	96	97	98	99	100

1	2	3	4	5	6	7	8	9	10
11	12	13	14	15	16	17	18	19	20
21	22	23	24	25	26	27	28	29	30
			34	35	36	37	38	39	40
41	42	43	44	45	46	47	48	49	50

31   32   33

4

51	52	53	54	55	56	57	58	59	60
61	62	63	64	65	66	67	68	69	70
71	72	73	74	75		77	78	79	80
81	82	83	84	85		87	88	89	90
91	92	93	94	95		97	98	99	100

75   76   77

76   86   90

76   86   96

Directions Have students: **3** color the boxes of the numbers as they count aloud by ones, starting at the yellow box and ending at the red box; **4** count forward, and then draw a circle around the row that shows the missing set of numbers.

© Pearson Education, Inc. K   **Topic 11** | Reteaching

Name _____

1 ⭐

Ⓐ 60

Ⓑ 70

Ⓒ 80

Ⓓ 90

2 🍎

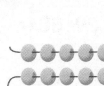
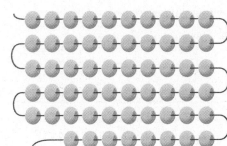

Ⓐ 56

Ⓑ 57

Ⓒ 58

Ⓓ 59

3 ↩

61	62	63	64	65	66	67	68	69	70
71	72	73	74	75	76	77	78	79	
81	82	83	84	85	86	87	88	89	
91	92	93	94	95	96	97	98	99	

Ⓐ 80 90 100

Ⓑ 80 80 99

Ⓒ 81 91 100

Ⓓ 85 95 100

Directions Have students mark the best answer. ⭐ Which number tells how many cubes? 🍎 Count the beads by tens and then by ones. Which number tells how many? ↩ Which set of numbers shows the set of missing numbers in the number chart?

4

1	2	3	4	5	6	7	8	9	10
11	12	13	14	15	16	17	18	19	20
21	22	23	24	25	26	27	28	29	30

 5

51	52	53	54	55	56	57	58	59	60
61	62	63	64	65	66	67	68	69	70
71	72	73	74	75	76	77	78	79	80
81	82	83	84	85	86	87	88	89	90
91	92	93	94	95	96	97	98	99	100

6

1	2	3	4	5	6	7	8	9	10
11	12	13	14	15	16	17	18	19	20
21	22	23	24	25	26	27	28	29	30
31	32	33	34	35	36	37	38	39	40
41	42	43	44	45	46	47	48	49	50
51	52	53	54	55	56	57	58	59	60
61	62	63	64	65	66	67	68	69	70
71	72	73	74	75	76	77	78	79	80
81	82	83	84	85	86	87	88	89	90
91	92	93	94	95	96	97	98	99	100

 7

11	12	13	14	15		17	18	19	
21		23	24	25	26	27	28	29	
31	32		34	35	36	37	38		
	42	43	44	45	46			49	50
51	52	53	54			57	58	59	60

21	22	28	30
33	35	39	40
41	46	47	48
51	55	56	60

Directions Have students: **4** color the boxes of the numbers that have the number *eight* in the ones place; **5** look at the row beginning with 61. Have them draw a circle around the tens place of the numbers to show the pattern, and then draw a circle around the column that has 0 in the ones place; **6** color the boxes of the numbers as they count by ones, starting at the yellow box and ending at the red box, and then explain any patterns they might see or hear; **7** count by ones to write the missing numbers in the top row, and then draw a circle around the missing numbers in the remaining rows.

© Pearson Education, Inc. K

Topic 11 | Assessment

 1

1	2	3	4	5	6	7	8	9	10
11	12	13	14	15	16	17	18	●	20
21	22	23	24	25	26	27	28	29	30
31	32	33	34	35	36	37	38	39	40
41	42	43	44	45	46	47	48	49	50

9   19   20

 2

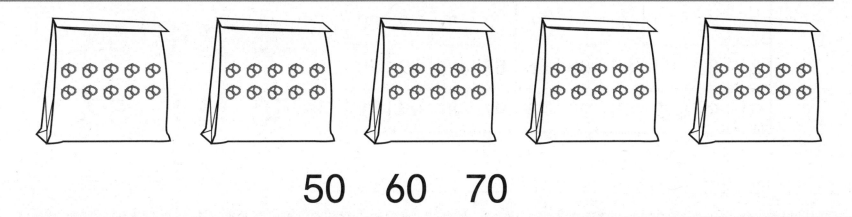

50   60   70

Directions **School Snacks** Say: *It's snack time for the Kindergarten class!* 1 Say: *Keisha puts a grape on the hundred chart to show how many grapes she has in her snack bag.* Have students look at the numbers that come just before and just after the grape, and then at the numbers that are just above and just below it. Have them draw a circle around the missing number that tells how many grapes Keisha has. 2 Have students count the pretzels that Liam and his friends share for their snack. Have them draw a circle around the number that tells how many. If needed, students can use the hundred chart to help.

❸

65   66   67

---

❹

❺

51	52	🍒	🍒	🍒	56	57	58	59	60
61	62	63	64	65	66	67	68	69	70
71	72	73	74	75	76	77	78	79	80
81	82	83	84	85	86	87	88	89	90
91	92	93	94	95	96	97	98	99	100

50   60   70

53   54   55

50   51   52

Directions ❸ Say: *Chen brings crackers for snack time. How many does he bring?* Have students draw circles around groups of crackers for easy counting by tens and ones. Then have them draw a circle around the number that tells how many. ❹ Say: *Zoe counts the cherries that she gives to her friends. She puts cherries on the number chart for the last three numbers that she counts.* Have students find the cherries in the chart. Then have them look at the numbers to the right of the chart, and then draw a circle around the set of missing numbers to show how Zoe counted the cherries. ❺ Say: *Ty has 64 raisins in one bag. He has 18 raisins in another bag. Help Ty count his raisins.* Have students start at 64 on the number chart and make a path to show how to count up 18 in any way they choose. Then have them draw a circle around the number where they stopped, and then explain how they counted up.

674 six hundred seventy-four   © Pearson Education, Inc. K   **Topic 11** | Performance Assessment

Identify and Describe Shapes

Essential Question: How can two- and three-dimensional shapes be identified and described?

Digital Resources

Solve Learn Glossary

Tools Assessment Help Games

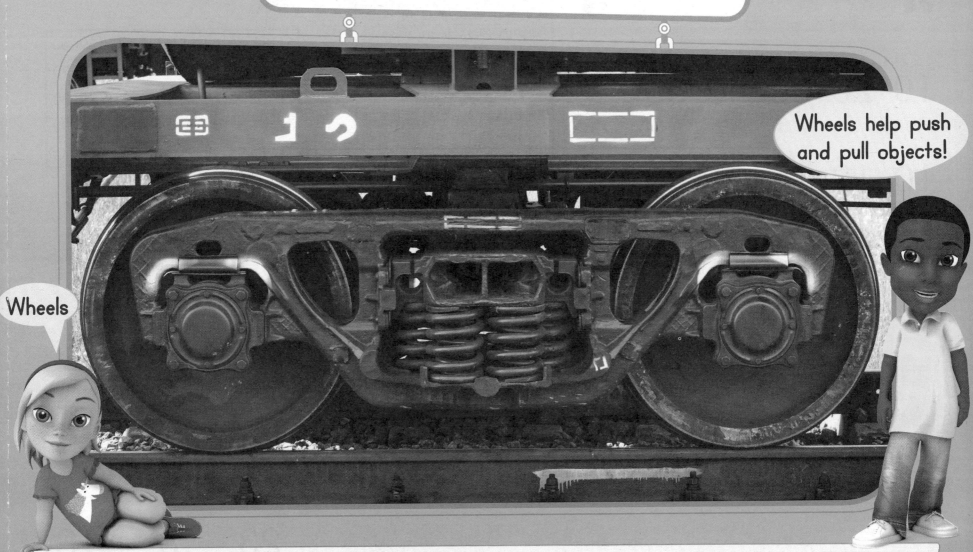

Wheels help push and pull objects!

Wheels

Math and Science Project: Pushing and Pulling Objects

Directions Read the character speech bubbles to students. **Find Out!** Have students investigate different kinds of wheels. Say: *Not all wheels look alike, but they are all the same shape. Talk to your friends and relatives about the shape of a wheel and ask them how it can help when you need to push and pull objects.* **Journal: Make a Poster** Have students make a poster that shows various objects with wheels. Have them draw up to 5 different kinds of objects that have wheels.

Name _____

Review What You Know

1

10 20 30 40 50

10 12 15 21 30

2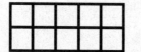

1	2	3	4	5	6	7	8	9	10
11	12	13	14	15	16	17	18	19	20
21	22	23	24	25	26	27	28	29	30
31	32	33	34	35	36	37	38	39	40
41	42	43	44	45	46	47	48	49	50
51	52	53	54	55	56	57	58	59	60
61	62	63	64	65	66	67	68	69	70
71	72	73	74	75	76	77	78	79	80
81	82	83	84	85	86	87	88	89	90
91	92	93	94	95	96	97	98	99	100

3

51	52	53	54	55	56	57	58	59	60
61	62	63	64	65	66	67	68	69	70
71	72	73	74	75	76	77	78	79	80
81	82	83	84	85	86	87	88	89	90
91	92	93	94	95	96	97	98	99	100

4

_____   _____

5

- - - - - - - - -

6

23   8   13

Directions Have students: **1** draw a circle around the set of numbers that show a pattern of counting by tens; **2** draw a circle around the hundred chart; **3** draw a circle around the numbers *fifty-five* and *ninety-nine*; **4** count the objects, write the numbers, and then draw a circle around the number that is greater than the other number; **5** count the objects, and then write the number; **6** draw a circle around the number that tells how many counters.

Topic 12

My Word Cards

Directions Have students cut out the vocabulary cards. Read the front of the card, and then ask them to explain what the word or phrase means.

sort

two-dimensional shape

three-dimensional shape

circle

triangle

side

My Word Cards

Directions Review the definitions and have students study the cards. Extend learning by having students draw pictures for each word on a separate piece of paper.

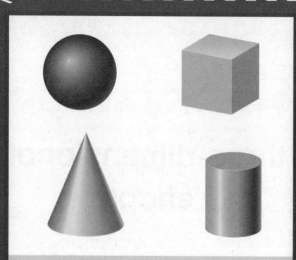

Point to the shapes.
Say: *Solid figures are also called* **three-dimensional shapes**.

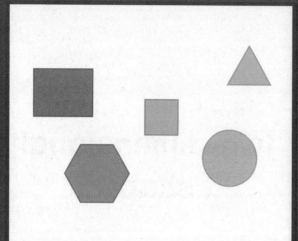

Point to the shapes.
Say: *Flat shapes are also called* **two-dimensional shapes**.

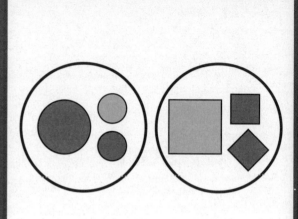

Point to the groups.
Say: *You can* **sort** *objects by shape.*

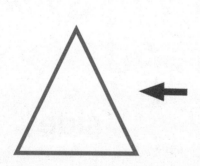

Point to the side of the triangle.
Say: *This is one* **side** *of the triangle. It has 3 sides in all.*

Point to the shape.
Say: *This shape is a* **triangle**.

Point to the shape.
Say: *This shape is a* **circle**.

© Pearson Education, Inc. K

My Word Cards

Directions Have students cut out the vocabulary cards. Read the front of the card, and then ask them to explain what the word or phrase means.

A-Z
Glossary

vertex (vertices)

square

rectangle

hexagon

sphere

cube

My Word Cards

Point to the shape.
Say: *This shape is a **rectangle**.*

Point to the shape.
Say: *This shape is a **square**.*

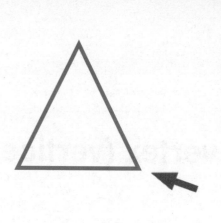

Point to the vertex of the triangle.
Say: *Another word for corner is **vertex**. All triangles have 3 **vertices**.*

Point to the shape.
Say: *This solid figure is a **cube**.*

Point to the shape.
Say: *This solid figure is a **sphere**.*

Point to the shape.
Say: *This shape is a **hexagon**.*

My Word Cards

Directions Have students cut out the vocabulary cards. Read the front of the card, and then ask them to explain what the word or phrase means.

A-Z Glossary

cone	cylinder	in front of
behind	next to	above

My Word Cards

Point to the orange.
Say: *The orange is **in front of** the basket.*

Point to the shape.
Say: *This solid figure is a **cylinder**.*

Point to the shape.
Say: *This solid figure is a **cone**.*

Point to the picture.
Say: *The picture is **above** the table.*

Point to the white dog.
Say: *The white dog is **next to** the brown dog.*

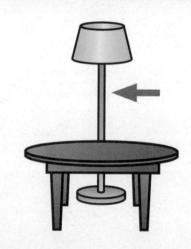

Point to the lamp.
Say: *The lamp is **behind** the table.*

My Word Cards

Directions Have students cut out the vocabulary cards. Read the front of the card, and then ask them to explain what the word or phrase means.

A-Z
Glossary

✂

below

beside

My Word Cards

Point to the dog.
Say: *The dog is **beside** the dog house.*

Point to the ball.
Say: *The ball is **below** the table.*

Directions Say: *Pick 6 shapes from a bag. Put the shapes into two groups. Tell how the groups are different. Then draw a picture of the shapes you put on each table.*

I can ...
name shapes as flat or solid.

I can also look for patterns.

Learn   Glossary

flat

STOP

solid

☆ Guided Practice

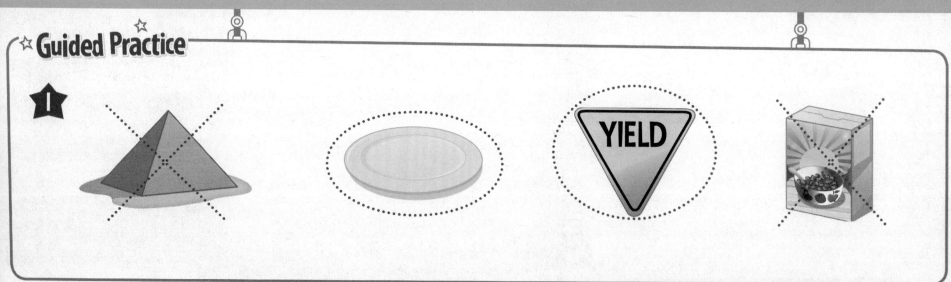

1.

YIELD

Directions ★ Have students draw a circle around the objects that are flat, and mark an X on the objects that are solid.

© Pearson Education, Inc. K

Name

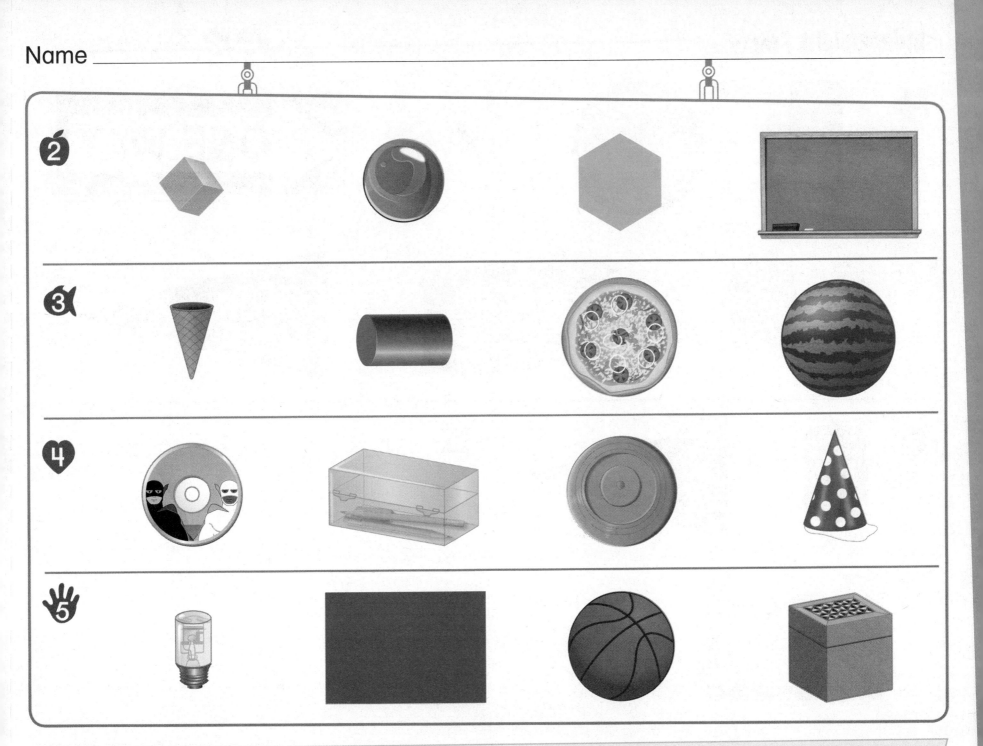

Directions Have students: ❷ and ❸ draw a circle around the objects that are flat in each row, and then mark an X on the objects that are solid; ❹ mark an X on the objects that are NOT flat; ❺ mark an X on the objects that are NOT solid.

Independent Practice

6

 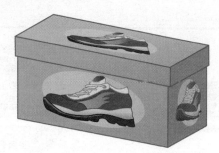 

7

8

Directions Have students: **6** mark an X on the objects that are solid. Then have them draw a circle around the objects that are flat; **7** mark an X on the objects that are NOT solid. **8 Higher Order Thinking** Have students draw a picture of an object that is solid.

       Topic 12 | Lesson 1

Name _____

Another Look!

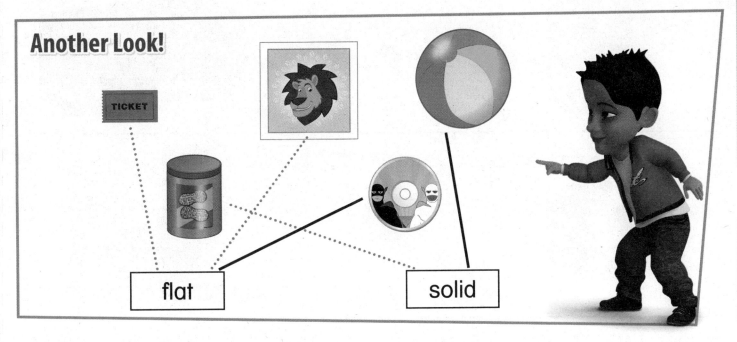

flat

solid

      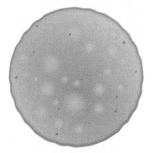

Directions Say: *The DVD is flat. What other objects are flat? Draw a line from the objects that are flat to the box labeled* flat. *The beach ball is solid. Draw a line from other objects that are solid to the box labeled* solid. ⭐ Have students draw a circle around the objects that are flat, and then mark an X on the objects that are solid.

2

3

4

5

Directions **2** and **3** Have students mark an X on the objects that are NOT flat. **4** **Higher Order Thinking** Have students identify an object in a bedroom that is solid, and then draw a picture of that object. **5** **Higher Order Thinking** Have students identify an object in a kitchen that is flat, and then draw a picture of that object.

Topic 12 | Lesson 1

Name _____

Solve

Directions Say: *The zoo has a polar animals exhibit. There are polar bears and penguins. Place the shapes in the animal pens that are the same shape. Tell how the shapes you placed in the pen on the left are different from the shapes you placed in the pen on the right.*

I can ...
identify and describe circles and triangles.

I can also look for patterns.

☆ Guided Practice

1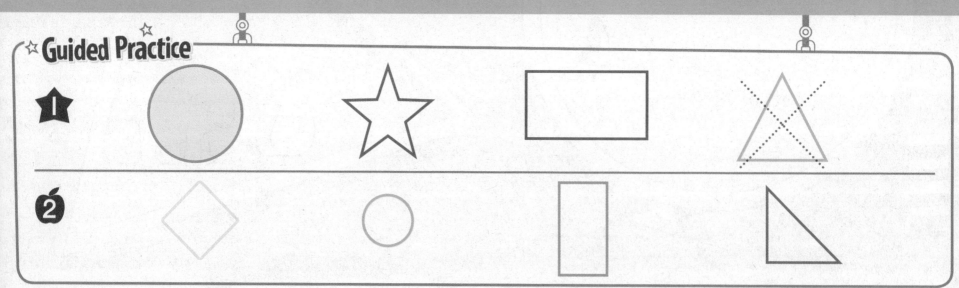

2

Directions 1 and 2 Have students color the circle in each row, and then mark an X on each triangle.

© Pearson Education, Inc. K

Topic 12 | Lesson 2

Name _____

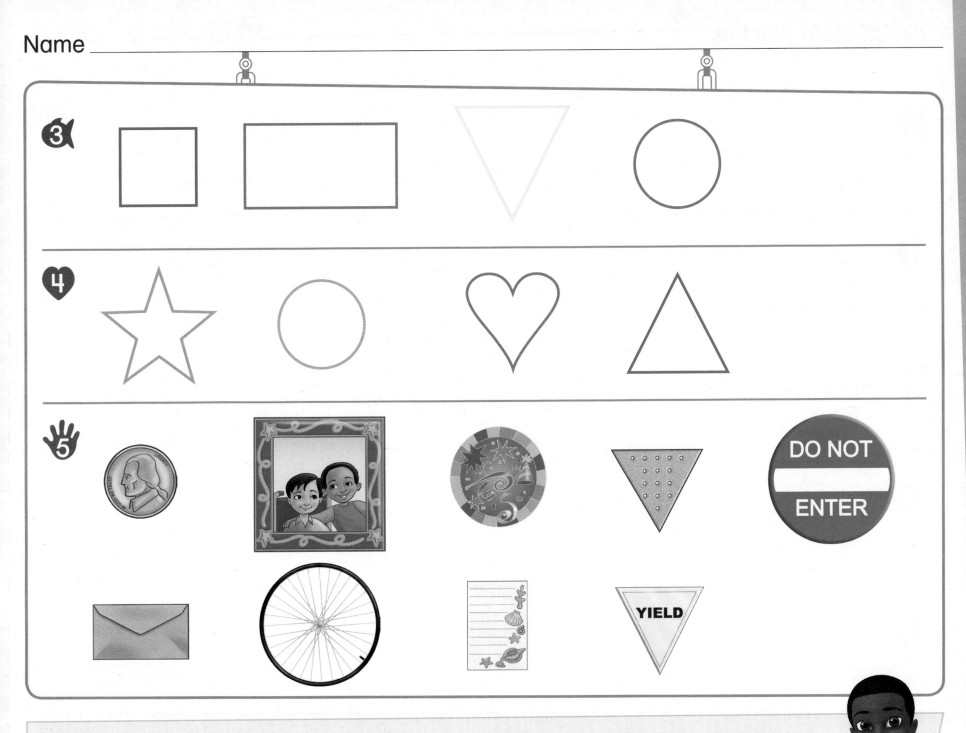

3

4

5

Directions ❸ Have students color the circle and mark an X on the triangle. ❹ **Number Sense** Have students mark an X on the shape that has 3 sides. ✋ Have students draw a circle around the objects that look like a triangle, and then mark an X on the objects that look like a circle.

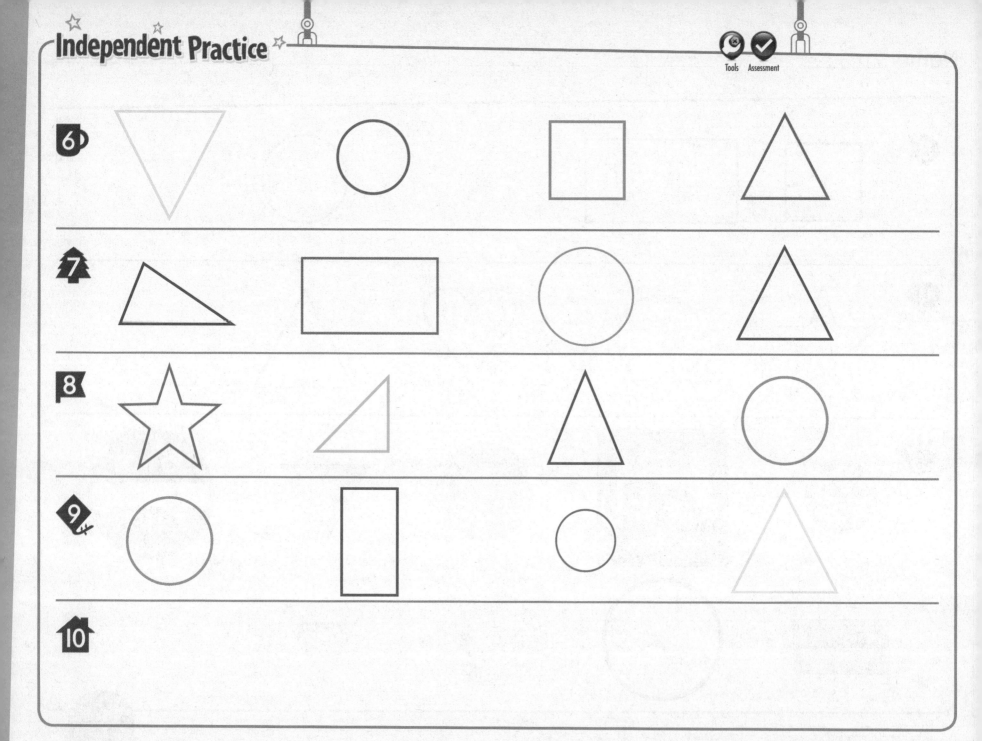

6 ▽ ◯ ▢ △

7 ◁ ▭ ◯ △

8 ☆ ◺ △ ◯

9 ◯ ▯ ◯ △

10

Directions 6–9 Have students color the circles and mark an X on the triangles in each row. **10 Higher Order Thinking** Have students draw a picture of an object that is shaped like a triangle.

© Pearson Education, Inc. K

Topic 12 | Lesson 2

Name _____

Another Look!

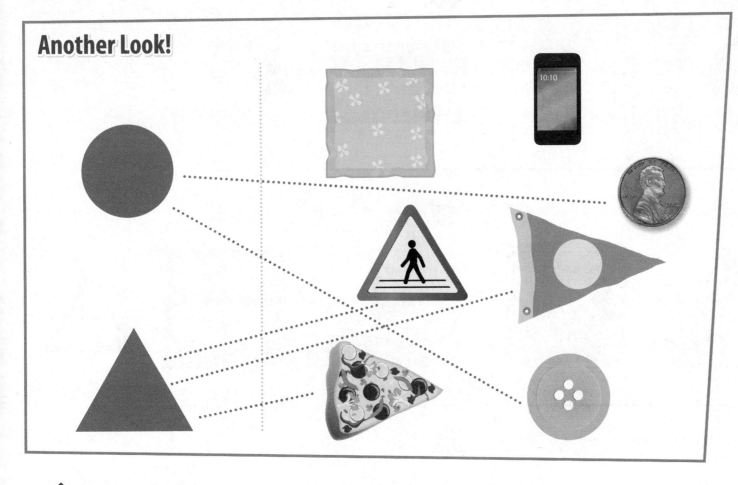

HOME ACTIVITY Look through a magazine with your child. Ask him or her to find pictures of objects that look like a circle or a triangle.

Directions Say: *A circle is round. Draw a line from the objects that look like a circle to the blue circle on the left. A triangle has 3 sides and 3 vertices. Draw a line from the objects that look like a triangle to the blue triangle on the left.* ⭐ *Have students draw a circle around the objects that look like a triangle and mark an X on the objects that look like a circle.*

2

 3

 4

 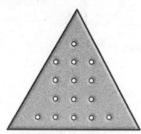 

 5

 6

 7

Directions Have students: **2** and **3** mark an X on the objects that look like a circle; **4** and **5** draw a circle around the objects that look like a triangle. **6 Higher Order Thinking** Have students draw a large red circle and a small blue triangle. **7 Higher Order Thinking** Have students draw a picture using at least 2 circles and 1 triangle. Have them tell a partner what they drew using the names of the shapes.

© Pearson Education, Inc. K **Topic 12** | Lesson 2

Name _____

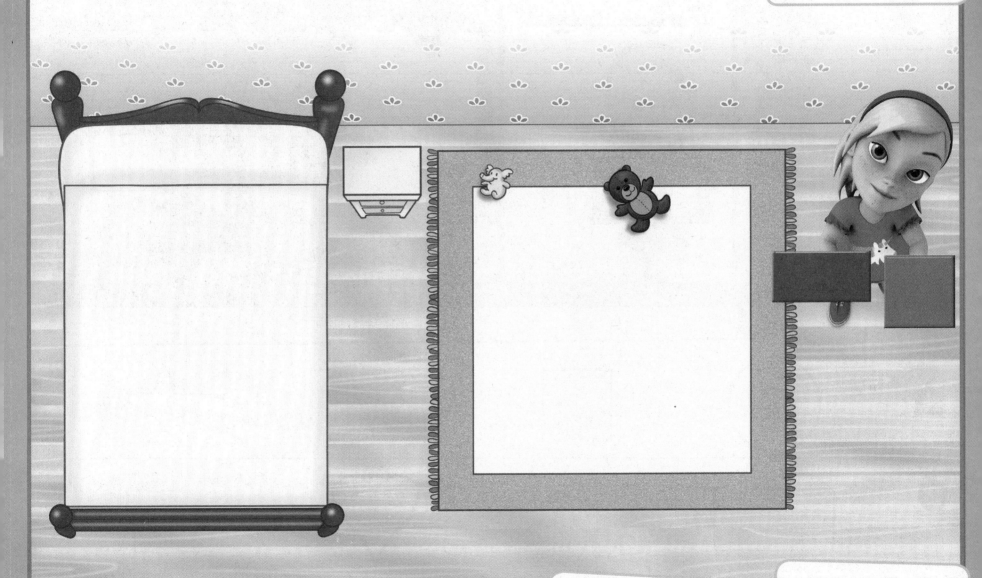

Directions Say: *Emily is holding 2 shapes. Pick either the red or the blue shape. Draw a line from that shape to something in the room that has the same shape.*

I can …
identify and describe squares and other rectangles.

I can also look for patterns.

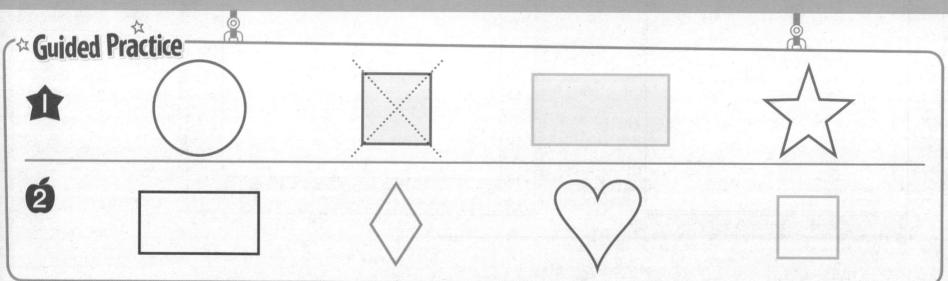

1

2

Directions ⭐ and 🍎 Have students color the rectangles in each row, and then mark an X on each rectangle that is also a square.

© Pearson Education, Inc. K

Name _____

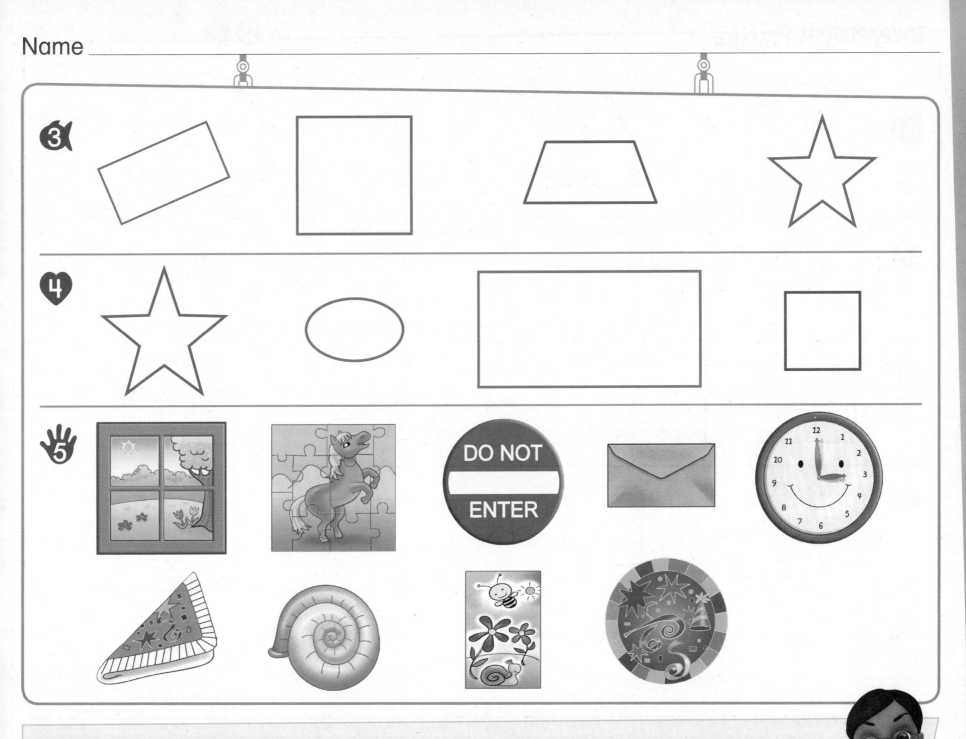

DO NOT
ENTER

Directions Have students: ❸ and ❹ color the rectangles in each row, and then mark an X on each rectangle that is also a square; ✋ draw a circle around the objects that look like a rectangle, and then mark an X on each object that also looks like a square.

Independent Practice

Tools   Assessment

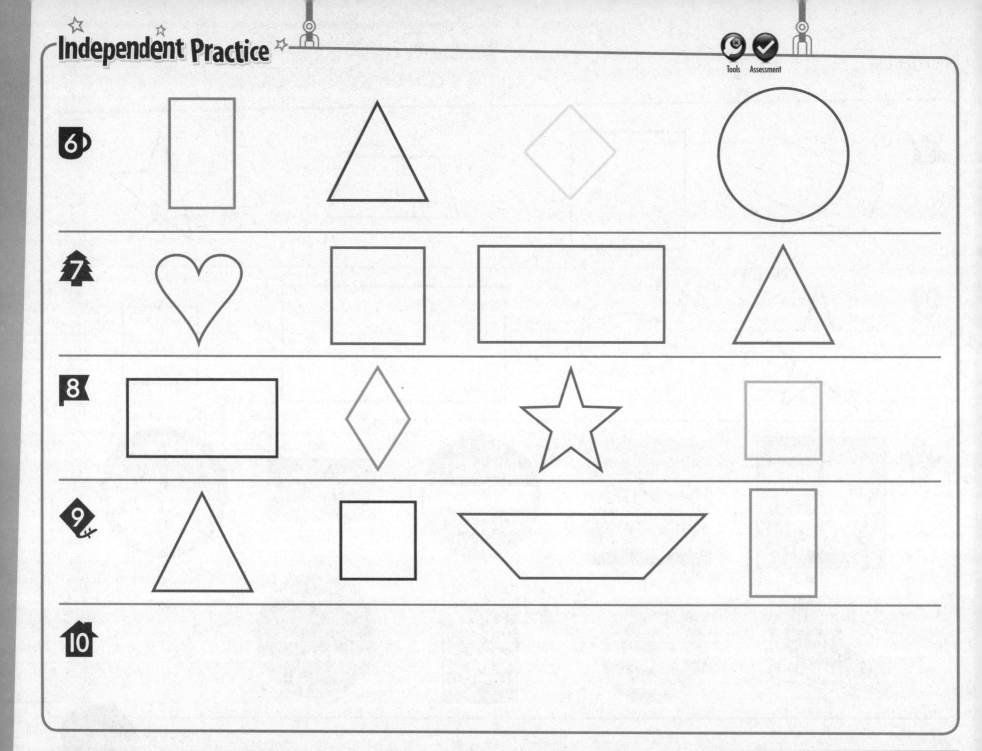

Directions ❻–❾ Have students color the rectangles in each row, and then mark an X on each rectangle that is also a square.
❿ **Higher Order Thinking** Have students draw a green rectangle, and then draw a yellow square.

700 seven hundred   © Pearson Education, Inc. K   **Topic 12** | Lesson 3

Name ________________________________

Help Tools Games

Homework & Practice 12-3

Squares and Other Rectangles

HOME ACTIVITY Take a walk around your home or neighborhood. Ask your child to look for windows that have the shape of a rectangle or a square.

Another Look!

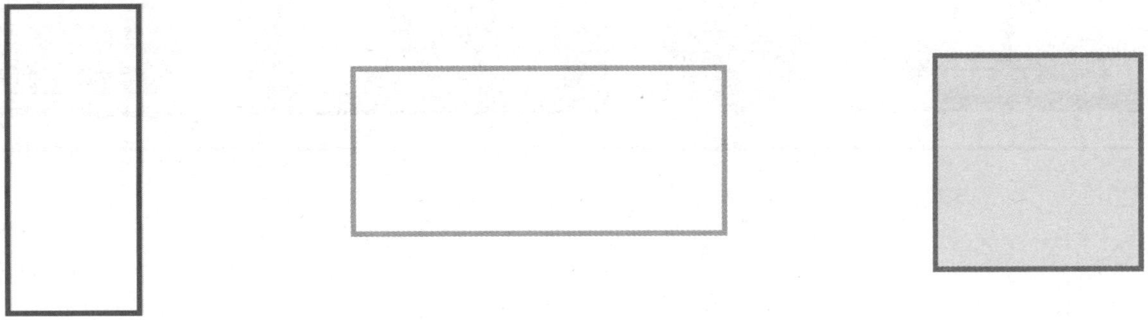

1

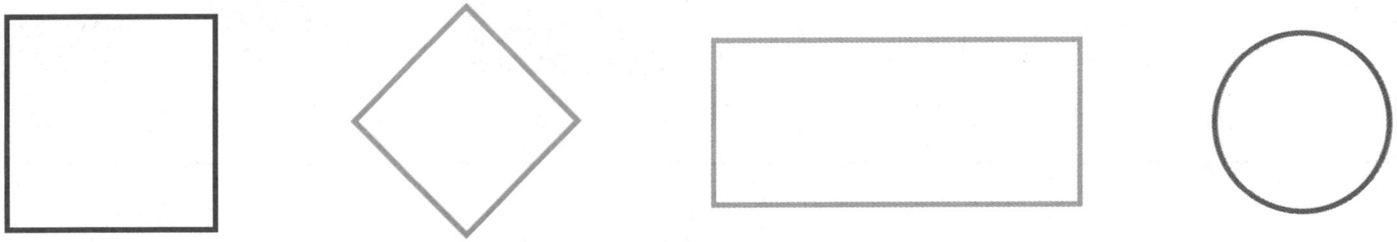

2

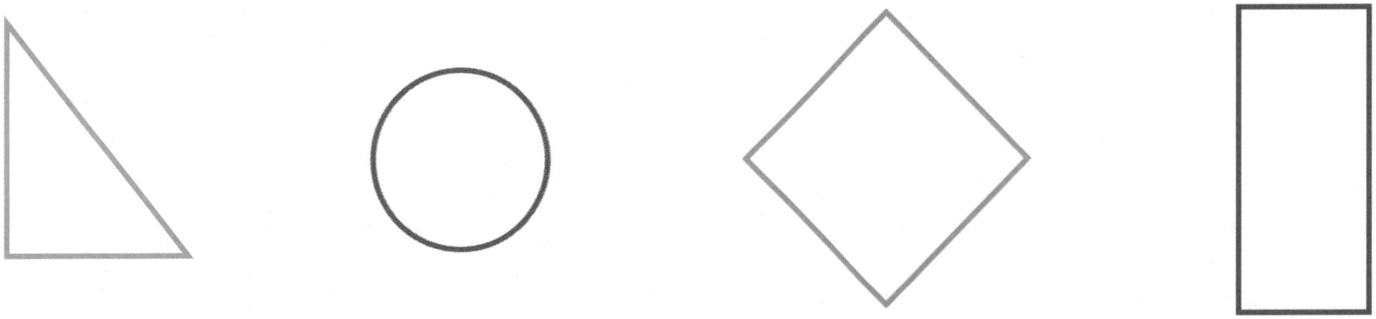

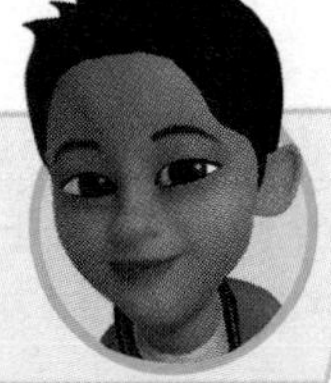

Directions Say: *Look at the shapes. What is the name of each shape? Color the square.* Have students: **1** look at the shapes, name them, and then color the squares; **2** look at the shapes, name them, and then color the rectangles.

3

 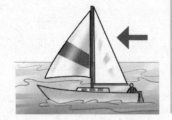

 4

 5

  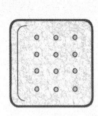   

6

 7

Directions Have students: **3** and **4** mark an X on the objects that look like a rectangle; **5** draw a circle around the objects that look like a square. **6 Higher Order Thinking** Have students draw an object that is both a rectangle and a square. **7 Higher Order Thinking** Have students draw a picture using at least 2 rectangles and 2 squares.

Topic 12 | Lesson 3

Solve & Share

Name _____

Solve

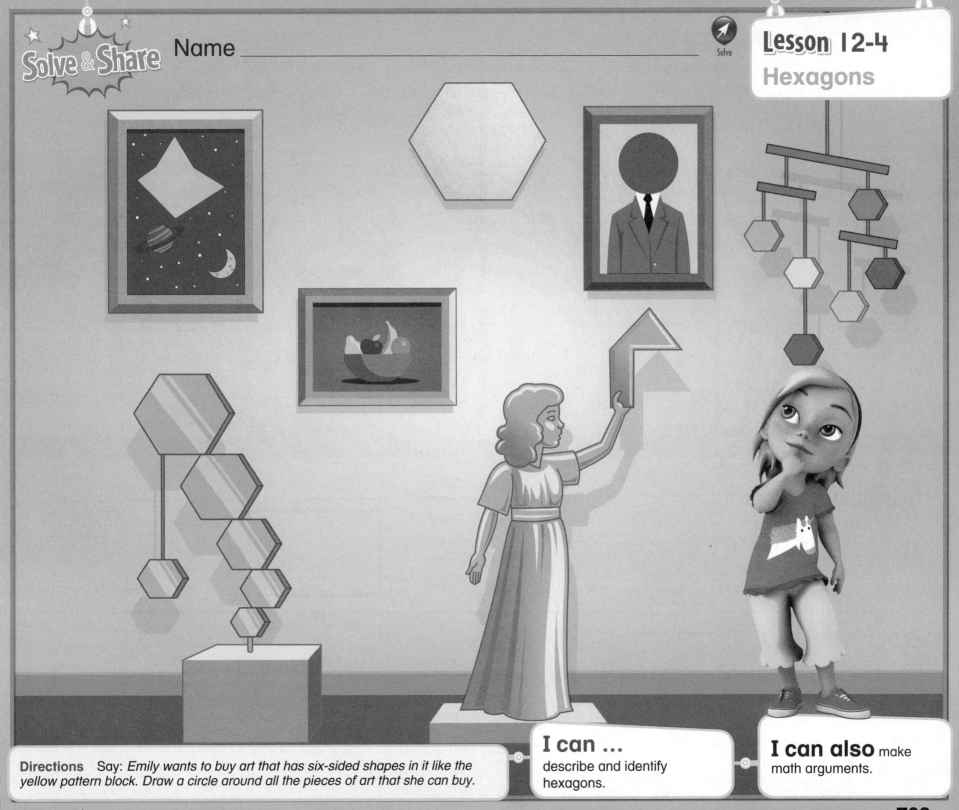

I can ...
describe and identify hexagons.

I can also make math arguments.

Directions Say: *Emily wants to buy art that has six-sided shapes in it like the yellow pattern block. Draw a circle around all the pieces of art that she can buy.*

☆ Guided Practice

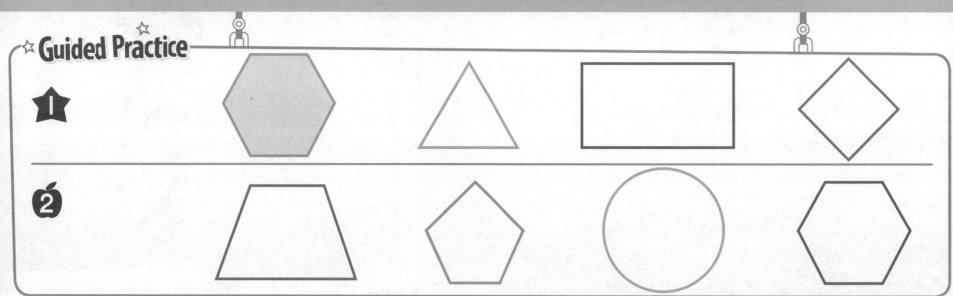

Directions ⭐ and ② Have students color the hexagon in each row.

Name _____

3 △ ⬡ ☆ ▢

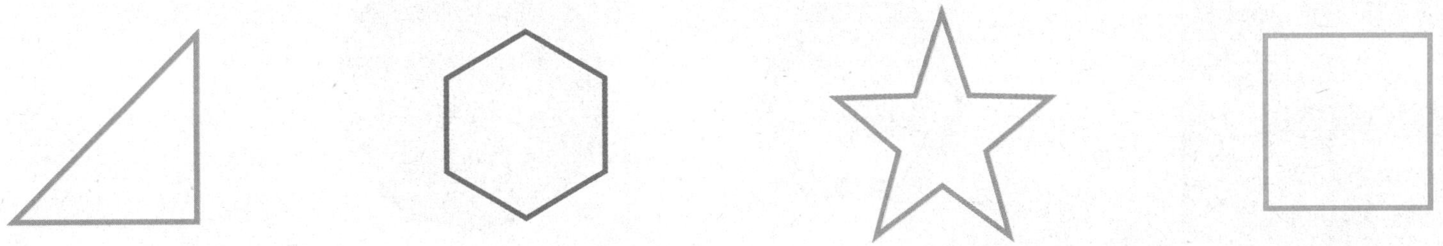

4 ♡ ▭ ⬡ ⬭

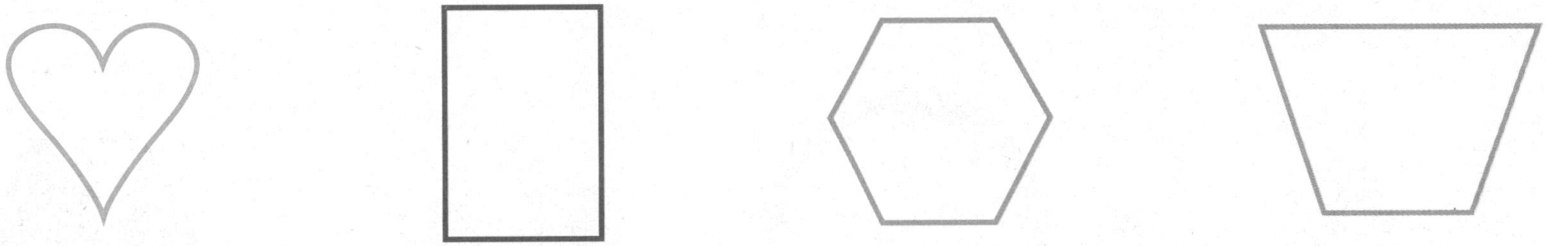

5 🍕 ⏺ 👜 ⬡

6 🐚 ⬡ 📔 ⛵

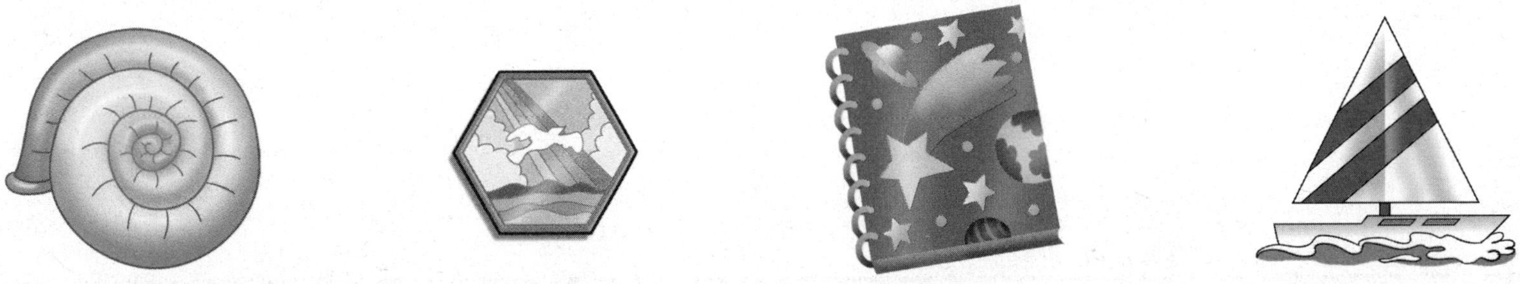

Directions Have students: **3** and **4** color the hexagon; **5** and **6** draw a circle around the object that looks like a hexagon.

Topic 12 | Lesson 4   seven hundred five   **705**

Independent Practice

7

8

Directions **7** Have students draw a circle around the objects that look like a hexagon. **8 Higher Order Thinking** Have students draw a picture using at least 1 hexagon.

Topic 12 | Lesson 4

Name _____

Another Look!

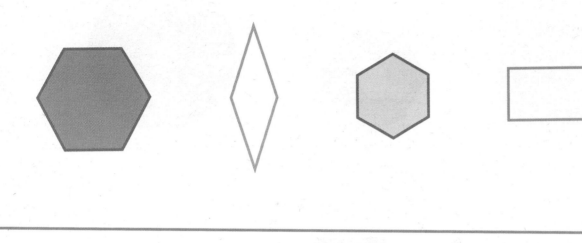

HOME ACTIVITY Have your child look through newspapers and magazines to identify pictures of objects that look like a hexagon. Then have them draw an object shaped like a hexagon.

  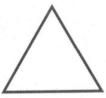

 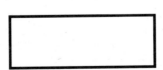  

Directions Say: *Look at the shapes. What is the name of each shape? Color the hexagons.* ★ and ❷ Have students color the hexagons in each row.

Directions ❸ and ❹ Have students draw a circle around the objects that look like a hexagon. ✋ **Higher Order Thinking** Have students draw a picture of an object that is shaped like a hexagon.

© Pearson Education, Inc. K

Topic 12 | Lesson 4

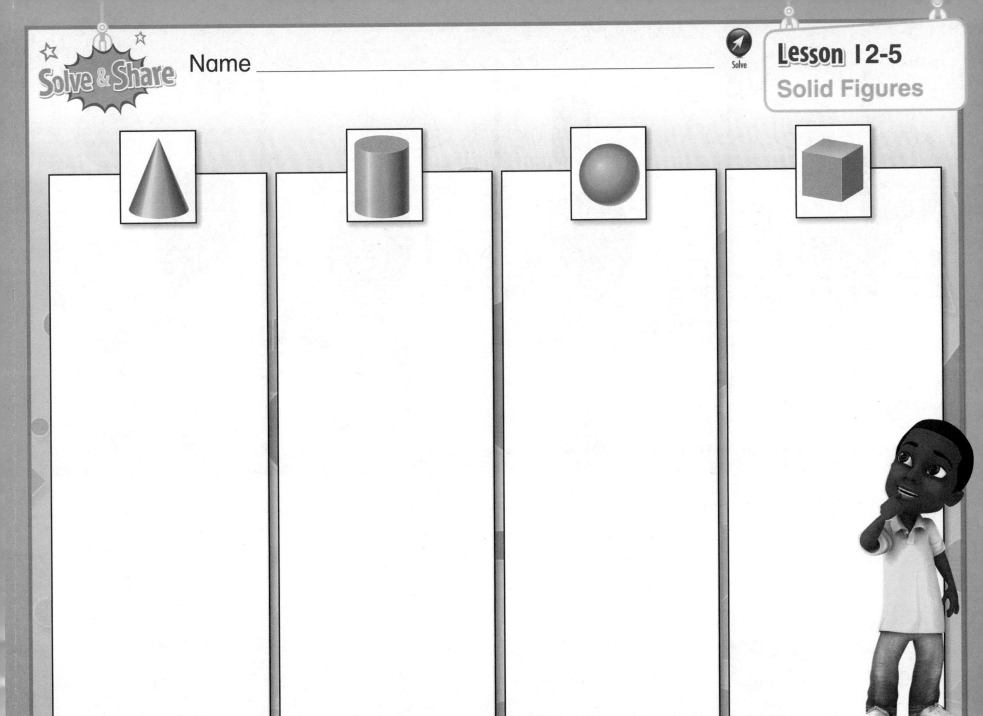

Directions Say: *Jackson wants to find objects that have the same shape as the solid figures. How can he find objects that have the same shape? Draw objects below each solid figure that have the same shape.*

I can ...
describe and identify solid figures.

I can also model with math.

Topic 12 | Lesson 5

Digital Resources at PearsonRealize.com

seven hundred nine **709**

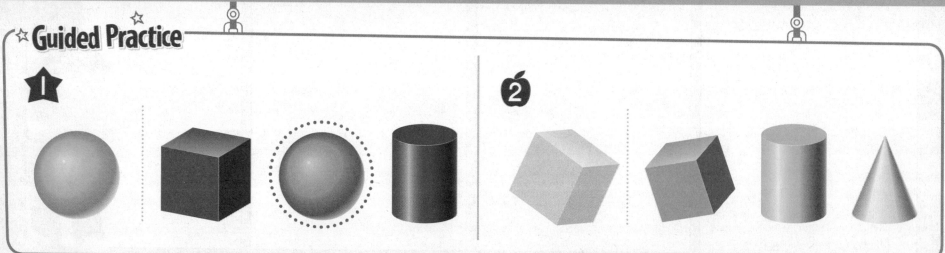

☆ Guided Practice

1

2

Directions **1** and **2** Have students name the solid figure on the left, and then draw a circle around the solid figure on the right that is the same shape.

© Pearson Education, Inc. K

Name _____

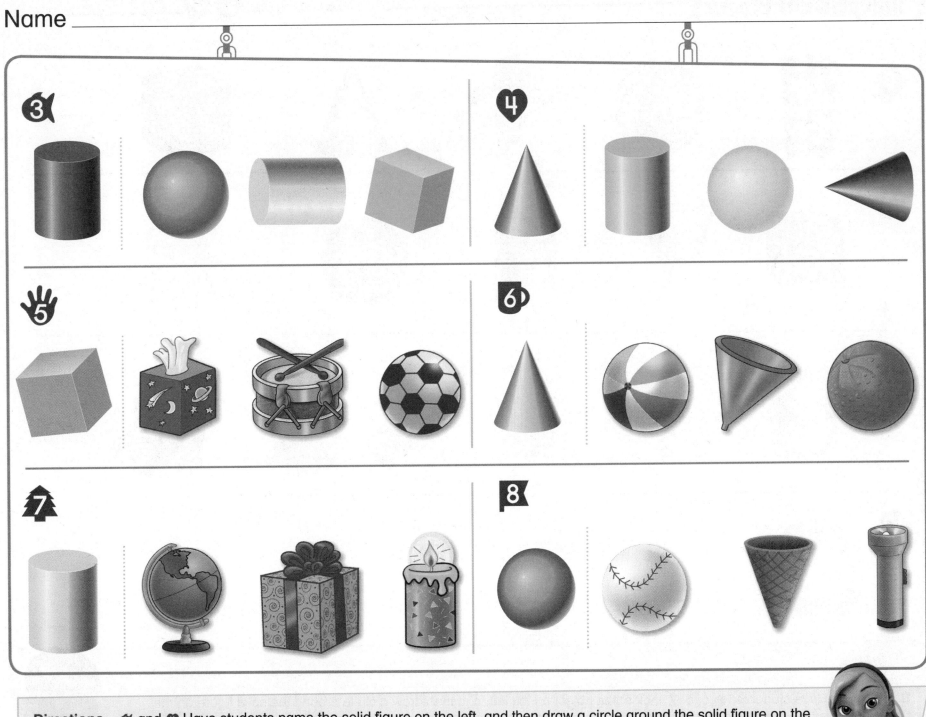

Directions ❸ and ❹ Have students name the solid figure on the left, and then draw a circle around the solid figure on the right that is the same shape. ❺—❽ Have students name the solid figure on the left, and then draw a circle around the object on the right that looks like that shape.

Independent Practice

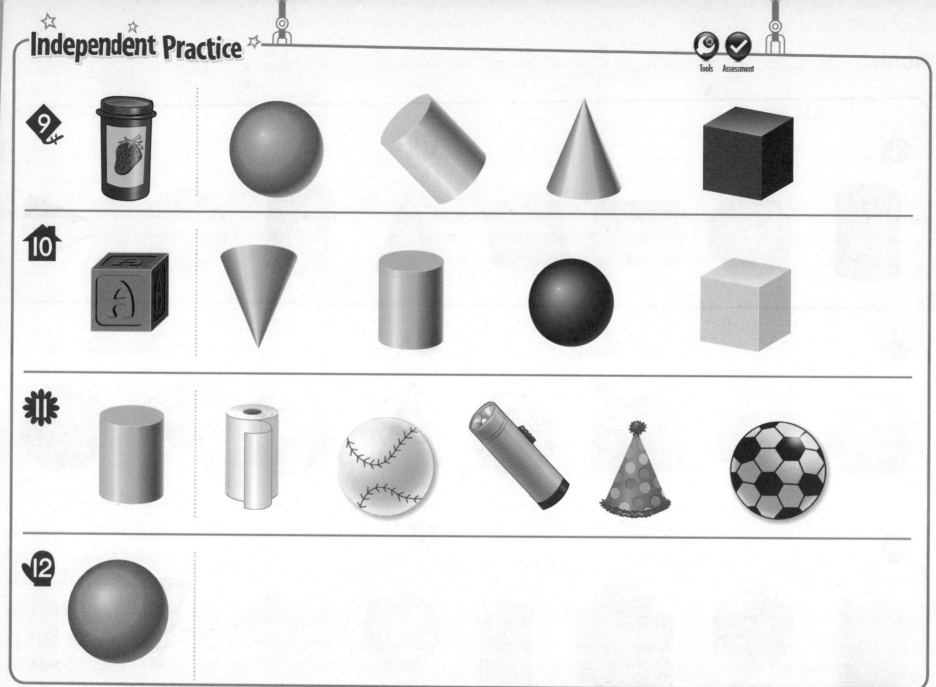

9

10

11

12

Directions Have students: **9** and **10** look at the object on the left, and then draw a circle around the solid figure on the right that looks like that shape; **11** name the solid figure on the left, and then draw a circle around the objects on the right that look like that shape. **12 Higher Order Thinking** Have students name the solid figure on the left, and then draw 2 more objects that look like that shape.

© Pearson Education, Inc. K

Topic 12 | Lesson 5

Name _____

Another Look!

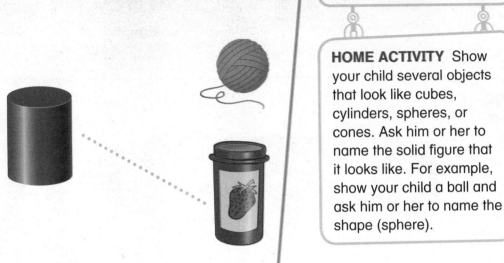

HOME ACTIVITY Show your child several objects that look like cubes, cylinders, spheres, or cones. Ask him or her to name the solid figure that it looks like. For example, show your child a ball and ask him or her to name the shape (sphere).

★1

 BEANS

2

Directions Have students point to the blue cone. Say: *This solid figure is a cone. Draw a line from the cone to the object that looks like that shape. Draw a line from the cylinder to the object that looks like that shape.* Have students: ★1 and 2 draw a line from each solid figure to the object that looks like that shape.

6

Directions ❸ and ❹ Have students draw a circle around the 4 objects in each row that look like the same shape, and then name the shape. ✋ **Math and Science** Say: *Pushing on an object can make it move. Some shapes are easier to push than others.* Have students draw a circle around the object that is easier to push. ❻ **Higher Order Thinking** Have students draw 2 objects that do NOT look like a sphere. Tell a partner what shapes the objects look like.

© Pearson Education, Inc. K
Topic 12 | Lesson 5

Directions Say: *Draw a circle around one of the shapes on the workmat. Name the shape. Can you find that shape in your classroom? Draw a picture of the object and its surroundings.*

I can ... describe shapes in the environment.

I can also look for patterns.

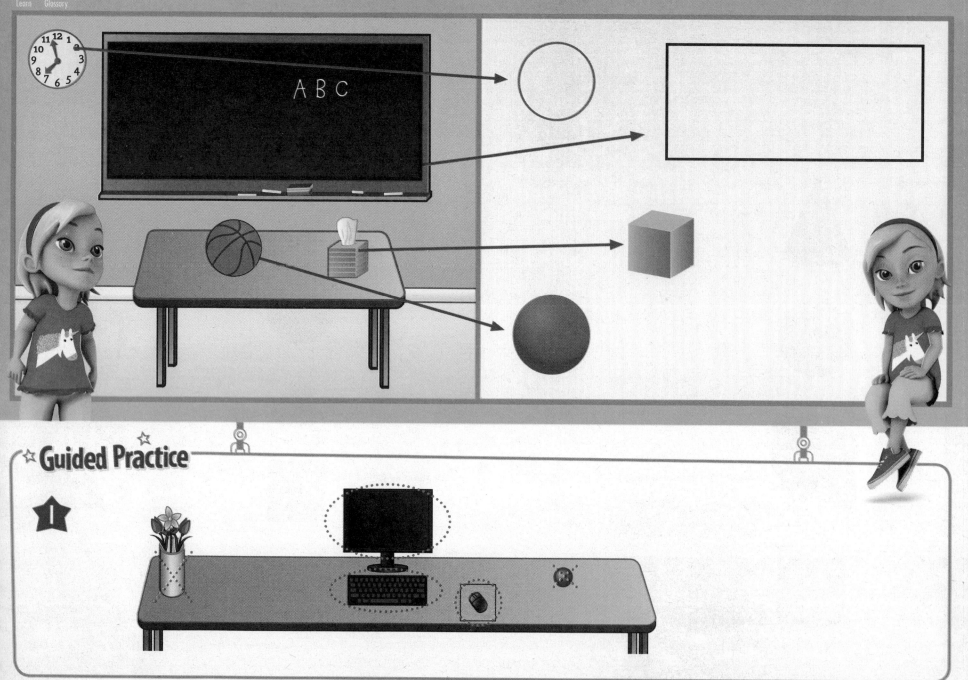

☆ Guided Practice

1

Directions ⭐ Have students point to objects in the picture and name their shape. Then have them draw a circle around objects that are flat, and then mark an X on the objects that are solid.

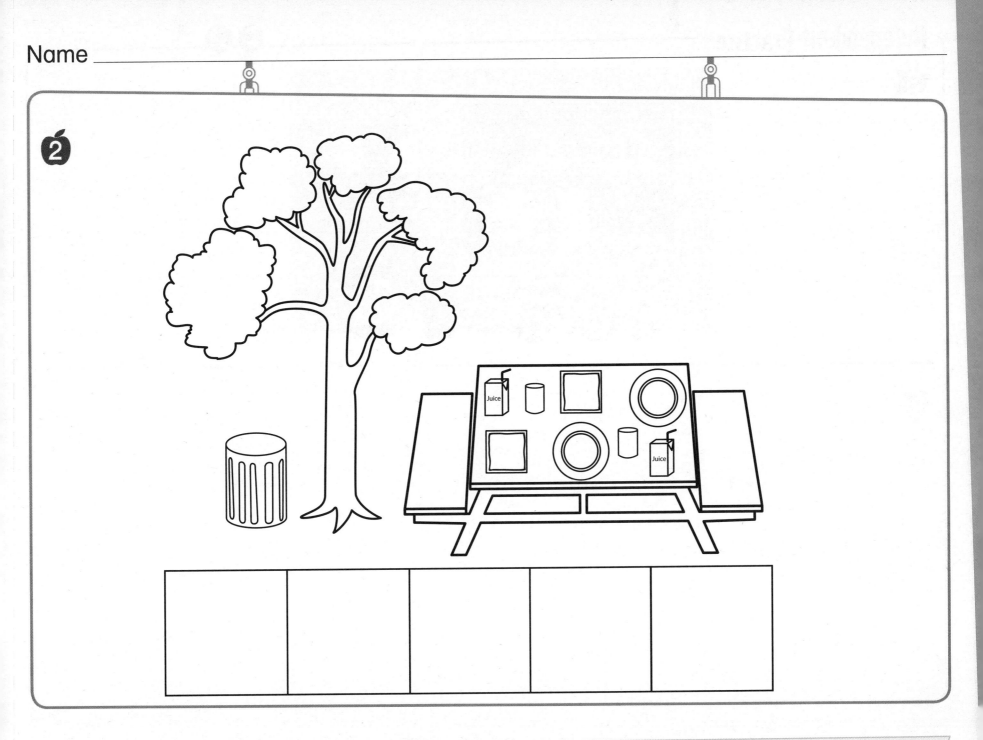

Directions ❷ **Vocabulary** Have students point to objects in the picture and name their shape. Then have them color the objects that look like a **square** blue, objects that look like a **cylinder** yellow, and objects that look like a **circle** red.

3

4

Directions **3** Have students point to objects in the picture and name each shape. Then have them draw a circle around the objects that look like a cylinder, and mark an X on the objects that look like a cone. **4** **Higher Order Thinking** Have students draw a picture of a park. Have them include 1 or more objects in the park that look like a rectangle.

718 seven hundred eighteen   © Pearson Education, Inc. K   **Topic 12** | Lesson 6

Name _____

Another Look!

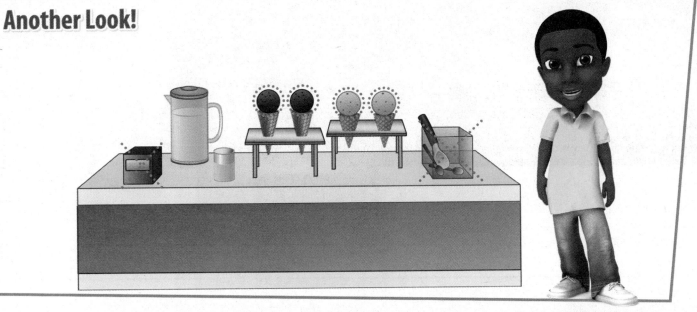

HOME ACTIVITY Have your child identify and name objects in your house that look like a circle, square, rectangle, triangle, hexagon, sphere, cube, cylinder, and cone. Have them tell where each object is located in the house.

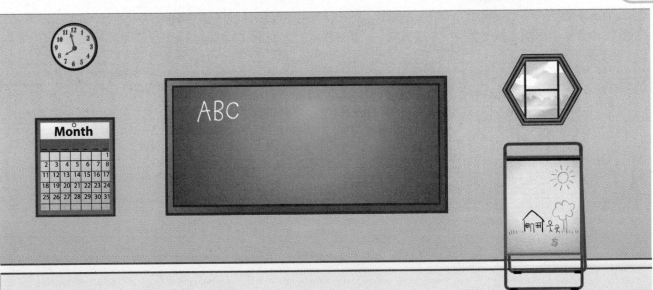

ABC

Month

Directions Say: *Point to a scoop of ice cream. What shape is the scoop of ice cream? Find other objects in the picture that look like a sphere and draw a circle around them. Can you find an object that looks like a cube? Mark an X on the objects that look like a cube.*
⭐ Have students point to objects in the picture and name each shape. Then have them draw a circle around the objects that look like a rectangle, and then mark an X on the object that looks like a hexagon.

Directions ❷ Have students point to objects in the picture and name their shape. Have them draw a circle around objects that are flat, and then mark an X on objects that are solid. ❸ **Higher Order Thinking** Have students draw a picture of a playground. Have them draw at least 1 object that looks like a sphere and 1 object that looks like a rectangle.

720 seven hundred twenty   © Pearson Education, Inc. K   **Topic 12** | Lesson 6

Name _____

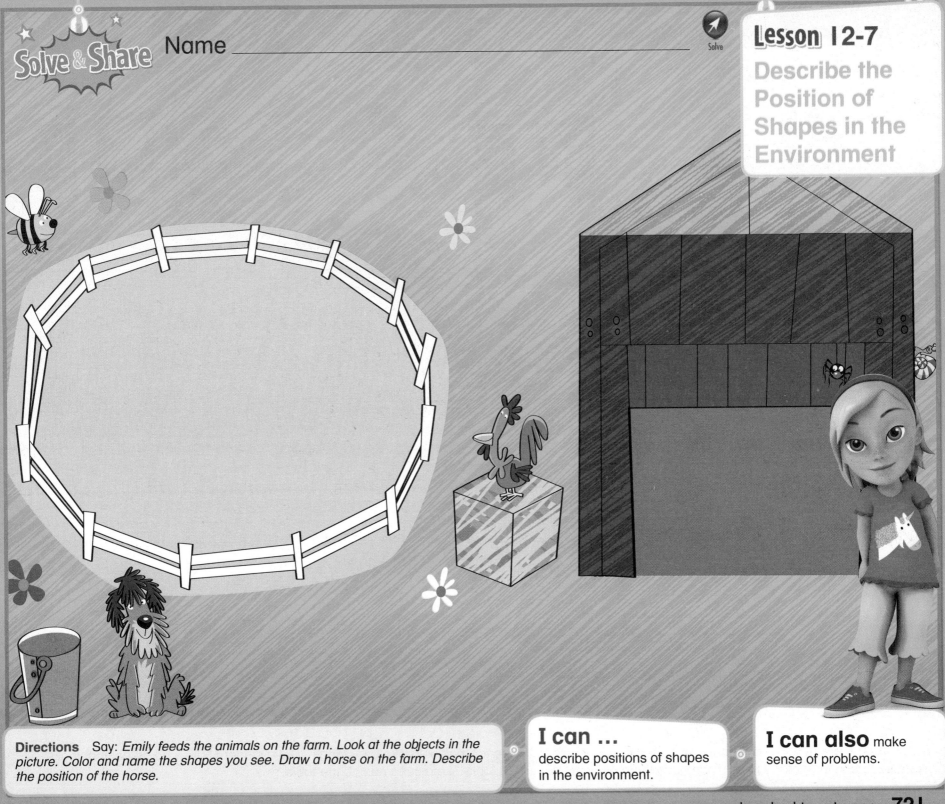

Directions Say: *Emily feeds the animals on the farm. Look at the objects in the picture. Color and name the shapes you see. Draw a horse on the farm. Describe the position of the horse.*

I can ... describe positions of shapes in the environment.

I can also make sense of problems.

Digital Resources at PearsonRealize.com

seven hundred twenty-one **721**

☆ Guided Practice

⭐ **1**

Directions ⭐ Have students mark an X on the object next to the pencil that looks like a rectangle. Have students draw an object that looks like a square in front of the mug. Then have them draw an object that looks like a cone next to the table.

Name _____

Directions ❷ Have students name the shape of the objects in the picture and use position words to describe their location. Then have them draw an X on the object in front of the sandcastle that looks like a cylinder. Have students draw an object that looks like a sphere beside Jackson, and then an object that looks like a rectangle beside the sandbox.

Tools Assessment

3

Directions ❸ **Higher Order Thinking** Have students mark an X on the object below the tree that looks like a rectangle. Have students draw an object that looks like a sphere above the tree, and then an object that looks like a triangle behind the fence. Then have them name the shape of the objects in the picture and use position words to describe their location.

     Topic 12 | Lesson 7

Name _____

Another Look!

City Park

HOME ACTIVITY Have your child name the shapes of several items in the kitchen, and then tell where they are located using the following position words: *above, below, in front of, behind, next to,* and *beside.*

Directions Say: *Look at the shapes on the left. Then look at the picture. Find the object that is below the tree, and then mark an X on the shape that it looks like. Then draw circles around the objects in the picture that look like circles.* ⭐ Have students find the object that is behind the cone, and then mark an X on the solid figure that it looks like on the left. Then have students draw circles around the objects in the picture that are shaped like spheres.

2

3

Directions ② Have students find the object that is above the table, and then mark an X on the solid figure that it looks like on the left. Then have students draw circles around the objects in the picture that are shaped like spheres. ③ **Higher Order Thinking** Have students draw an object shaped like a cube below an object shaped like a sphere, and beside an object shaped like a cone.

© Pearson Education, Inc. K

Topic 12 | Lesson 7

Name _____

Think.

Directions Say: *Emily's teacher teaches her class a game. She uses 1 blue cube, 1 red cube, 1 yellow counter, and 1 red counter and puts each of them somewhere on the farm picture. Play this game with a partner. Place the tools on the page, and then describe where one of them is located. Do NOT tell your partner which one you are talking about. How can your partner tell which one you are describing? Change places and play again.*

I can ... describe positions of shapes in the environment.

I can also name shapes correctly.

☆ Guided Practice

1

Directions ⭐ Have students mark an X on the object above the bed that looks like a cube. Then have them explain how they know they are correct. Then have them draw a shape that looks like a rectangle next to the bed.

Name _____

Independent Practice

 2

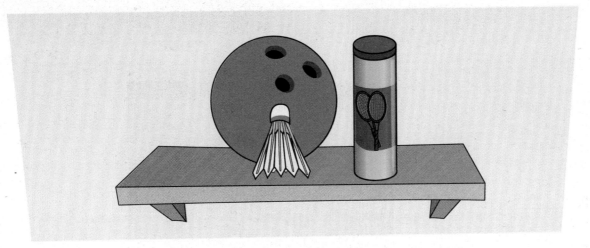

 3

Directions ❷ Have students name the shapes of the objects in the picture. Then have them mark an X on the object that is behind another object, and is next to the object that looks like a cylinder. Have them explain how they decided which shape to mark. ❸ Have students find the object in the picture that is NOT beside the box of tissues, and then mark an X on the solid it looks like on the left. Have them explain why a sphere is NOT the right answer. Then have them name the shape of the objects in the picture.

Directions Read the problem to students. Then have them use multiple problem-solving methods to solve the problem. Say: *Carlos wants to tell a friend about different things in the locker room and where they are located. What words can he use?* ❹ **Be Precise** *Mark an X on the object that looks like a cylinder that is beside the object that looks like a cube. What words helped you find the correct object?* ✋ **Reason** *Carlos says the soccer ball is behind the water bottle. What is another way to explain where the water bottle is?* ❻ **Explain** *Carlos describes the rectangle poster as being above the circle clock. Do you agree or disagree? Explain how you know you are correct.*

Name _____

Another Look!

HOME ACTIVITY Place several items on a table, such as a plate, spoon, fork, cup, and napkin. Have your child tell the position of each object using the following words: *above, below, beside, next to, in front of,* and *behind.* For example, a child might say, "The spoon is beside the plate."

Directions Say: *Look at the objects in the picture. Name the shapes of the objects you see. Now draw a circle around the shapes that you see. Name the object above the basketball. Mark an X on that object. Draw a circle around the object that is next to the basketball and below the block.* ⭐ Have students mark an X on the object that looks like a sphere below the picnic table. Then have them draw a circle around the object that looks like a cylinder beside the tree.

Directions Read the problem to students. Then have them use multiple problem-solving methods to solve the problem. Say: *Marta wants to tell a friend about different things in the kitchen and where they are located. What words can she use?* ❷ **Be Precise** Mark an X on the object that looks like a cylinder that is behind the object that looks like a cone. What words helped you find the correct object? ❸ **Reason** The ice cream cone is next to the sugar cube. What is another way to explain where the ice cream cone is? ❹ **Explain** Marta describes the door as looking like a rectangle. She also says it is below the clock. Do you agree or disagree? Explain how you know you are correct.

© Pearson Education, Inc. K

⭐ 1

5 − 2	3 − 1	1 − 1	2 + 0	5 − 4
5 − 0	0 + 2	3 + 1	2 − 0	1 + 2
1 + 4	2 + 0	4 − 2	5 − 3	4 − 0
0 + 1	1 + 1	4 − 3	3 − 1	4 − 1
3 + 2	4 − 2	0 + 3	1 + 1	4 − 4

🍎 2

_____

— — — — — —

_____

Directions Have students: ⭐ color each box that has a sum or difference that is equal to 2; 🍎 write the letter that they see.

I can ...
add and subtract fluently within 5.

TOPIC 12 Vocabulary Review

A-Z Glossary

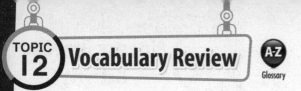

1

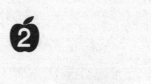

2

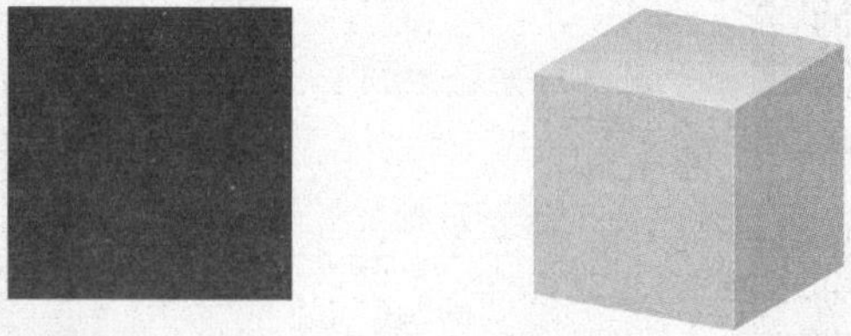

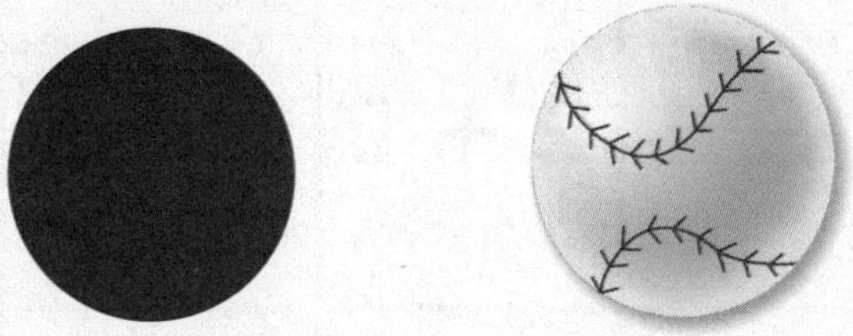

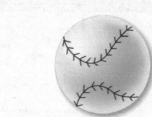

3

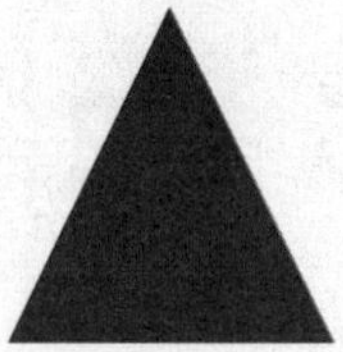

4

5

Directions **Understand Vocabulary** Have students: 1 draw a circle around the **two-dimensional** shape; 2 draw a circle around the **three-dimensional** shape; 3 draw a circle around the **vertices** of the triangle; 4 draw a **circle**; 5 draw a shape that is NOT a **square**.

Name _____

Set B

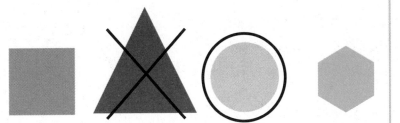   

Directions Have students: draw a circle around the objects that are flat, and then mark an X on the objects that are solid; draw a circle around the objects that look like a circle, and then mark an X on the objects that look like a triangle.

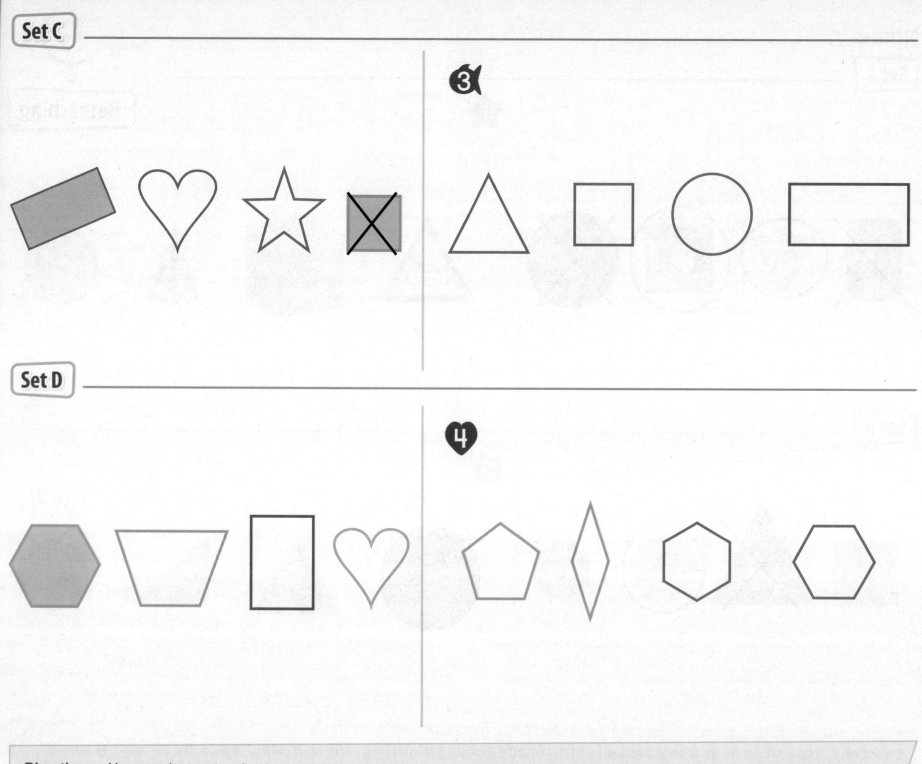

Directions Have students: ❸ color the rectangles, and then mark an X on the rectangle that is a square; ❹ color the hexagons.

736 seven hundred thirty-six   © Pearson Education, Inc. K   **Topic 12** | Reteaching

Name _____

_____

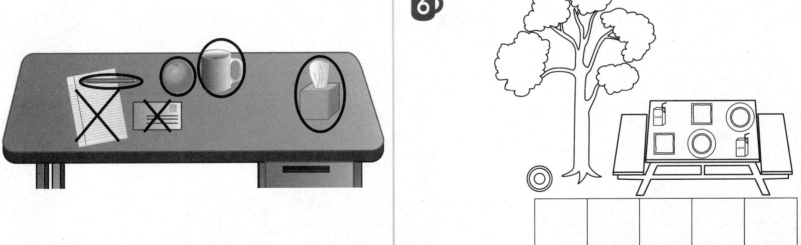

_____

Directions Have students: ✋ name the solid figure on the left, and then draw a circle around the solid figure that looks like that shape on the right; 🔟 point to each object in the picture and tell what shape each looks like. Then have them draw a circle around the objects that are solid, and mark an X on objects that are flat.

Directions Have students: **7** mark an X on the object that is next to the blue book, and then draw a circle around the object that is below the object that is shaped like a sphere; **8** mark an X on the objects that look like a circle that are behind the object that is shaped like a sphere.

Topic 12 | Reteaching

Name _____

 1

(A)

(B)

(C)  JACKSON ST

(D)

2

☐

☐

☐

☐

3

(A)

(B)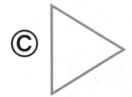

(C)

(D)

4

(A)

(B) CLOSED

(C)

(D)

Directions Have students mark the best answer. **1** Which object is NOT solid? **2** Mark all the objects that look like a hexagon. **3** Which object is NOT a triangle? **4** Which object looks like a square?

5

 6

  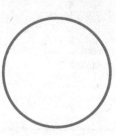

 7

Directions Have students: 🖐 mark an X on the objects that do NOT look like a circle; ☕ name the shapes, color the rectangles, and then mark an X on the rectangle that is a square; 🌲 look at the solid figure on the left, and then draw a circle around the object that looks like that shape.

Name _____

flat	solid

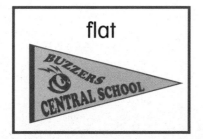

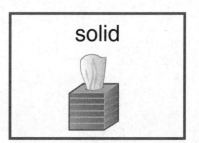

Directions Have students: 8 draw an object that looks like a cylinder in front of the vase. Then mark an X on the object that looks like a square next to the cat; 9 draw lines from the objects that are flat to the first box. Then have them draw lines from the objects that are solid to the second box.

Directions Have students: 🏠 draw a picture of an object that looks like a sphere below a book and next to a cup; ✹ draw a picture of an object that is flat. Then have them draw an object that is solid; ✌️ draw a circle around the objects that look like a circle, and then mark an X on the objects that look like a rectangle.

© Pearson Education, Inc. K **Topic 12** | Assessment

Name _____

1

2

Directions   Play Time! Say: *Supna and her friends are playing with toys.* Have students: **1** draw a circle around the toys that look like a cube. Have students mark an X on the toys that look like a cylinder; **2** draw a circle around the toys that look like a rectangle. Then have them mark an X on the rectangles that are squares.

Directions Have students: ③ mark an X on the object in the playroom that looks like a hexagon; ④ draw an object next to the shelves that looks like a cone; ✋5 listen to the clues, and then draw a circle around the object the clues describe. Say: *The object is above the blocks. It looks like a sphere. It is next to a green ball. The object is NOT yellow.*

© Pearson Education, Inc. K
Topic 12 | Performance Assessment